freefall

Living Life Beyond The Edge

sally anderson

NEW YORK

f r e e f a l l

Living Life Beyond The Edge

s a l l y   a n d e r s o n

ISBN 978-1-61448-085-3 Paper
ISBN 978-1-61448-086-0 eBook
Library of Congress Control Number: 2011933995

Published by:
MORGAN JAMES PUBLISHING
The Entrepreneurial Publisher
5 Penn Plaza, 23rd Floor
New York City, New York 10001
(212) 655-5470 Office
(516) 908-4496 Fax
www.MorganJamesPublishing.com

Interior Design by:
Bonnie Bushman
bbushman@bresnan.net

In an effort to support local communities, raise awareness and funds, Morgan James Publishing donates one percent of all book sales for the life of each book to Habitat for Humanity.
Get involved today, visit
www.HelpHabitatForHumanity.org.

For Roger, my Husband

Dreams Do Come True!

foreword

At the end of seminars, workshops or courses, feedback forms are circulated and everyone is asked to rate course content, catering, overall experience and much else. Apart from generating spurious data: 98%, of attendees rated it the best workshop they'd ever attended, 76% said it was outstanding value for money and other rubbish of this kind, these forms are only there to harvest complements. Catch people after an upbeat ending and you have to be pretty dreadful not to be knee deep in gushing praise to put on your website and clog up cyberspace. The pick of the crop can be cherry picked, edited to remove mild criticisms and used for marketing purposes. We all do it.

But Sally Anderson and her seminars deserve a more measured appraisal. After all she claims that she can do a lot in a short period and that her methods, if applied, are sustainable. And she doesn't come cheap.

Like many others who come to Sally, I've been around the block a few times. In my case was a psychiatric nurse for a quarter of a century, spending around 15 years as a group therapist, had about four years, twice weekly psychotherapy and must have attended hundreds of courses and teaching sessions which one way or another were related to mental health or human development. These courses have ranged from the sublime at one extreme to the seriously awful.

I'd say that Sally's course is up there with the best of them and Sally as an enabler is as effective as some of the best consultant psychiatrists and psychologists I've had the privilege to work with. She comes from a different place from the people I'm thinking about but like them she fuses theory with life experience and has a style built around her own personality rather than one borrowed from others.

And like the best people in this field, Sally loves difficult customers. She relishes working with the stroppy, the rude and the angry. She also likes the challenge of working with subversive, manipulative saboteurs: I know; I am one. That said it was interesting to witness how subtly she changed and adapted her methods for different delegates: she confronted everyone yet some were prompted more than others and she varied her pace depending on who was in front of her. I've been on courses where one senses that the facilitator has a favourite group member or favoured condition he or she likes to work with. I didn't for one moment get this feeling with Sally. I felt we were all valued equally. When leading a group there is always a danger that you can bully individuals or everyone but again I felt this didn't happen.

Where Sally most differs from psychiatrists, psychologists and psychiatric nurses I have worked with in the past is in the area of self-disclosure. Healthcare professionals are taught to disclose minimal personal information about themselves. The rationale is that patients will take an interest in the private lives of a therapist to avoid looking at their own issues and in psychotherapy it prevents a therapist understanding the "transference" that is going on. Personally I found the opposite to be true. The more directly I answered questions patients asked me the less interested in me they became and we could turn our attention back to where it belonged. But Sally goes way beyond this as she is an open book and keeps no secrets from course members. Being entrusted with this information compels everyone else to be equally revealing and the group bonds in no time at all and everyone works hard helping each other.

What did I get from attending the seminar? Apart from a lot of tools to help bits of me that are malfunctioning it is difficult to describe the relief of feeling that someone has finally got me. After decades of irritating, baffling, confusing, exasperating and undermining therapists and group leaders who were trying to help me it is wonderful to have more than met my match. Whether I use what I have been given is of course down to me, but I'm glad that the game playing is over. It was fun at the time but it's time to move on.

Peter Cross

Peter Cross is a journalist, writer, editor and former team co-ordinator of a dynamic UK psychiatric day hospital.

acknowledgments

To my Mom, Jude: I'm grateful to have been born into this family and I have never questioned your love; I know that everything that has happened was in perfection, and I love you beyond words.

To my Dad, Peter, who passed away January 2000: Miss you Dad, but I know you are with me every step of the way.

To my brother Mark, who passed away December 1983: Thank you for keeping me alive. In dying so early you became my savior.

To my brother Simon and Sister Kirstie: I love you and feel privileged to be your sister.

To Richard Dunbar & Neil Morgan: Thank you for always being there and teaching me the power of unconditional love and friendship.

To Megan Ruru: Know I am alive because of you.

To Gayel Marquet & Patterson Stark: Thanks for being the best cheer leaders ever; your support of Roger and I and this venture has been beyond extraordinary.

To Carol & Charlie Caldwell: You humble me with the significant contribution you have made to Roger and I.

To Sonya Nicol & Carolyn Bassett: Your unfailing support in co-creating this vision has been and continues to be extraordinary.

To Leanne Morris: Your loyalty and support both in business and in friendship has been amazing.

To Carleen & Sonny Cooper/Adaleen & Jack Griffith: Thank you for your support in the early stages of this venture.

To Gary Nuttall: You know what you have contributed and for that I am indebted.

To Carl Sowter: Thank you for believing in me and for your contribution to this venture.

To Trish Love: Thank you for teaching me what it means to be profoundly contributed to.

To Georgie & Michael Major: Your friendship means the world to me, thanks for always being there!

To Lisa Lark: Thank you for helping me find my voice.

To Lucille Burton: Thank you for your co-creative partnership in both business and in friendship

To Philby Brown: You will know what I mean when I say 'Love You More!'

To Angella Gilbert: You are an inspiration – thank you for all that you have contributed to me!

To Laurel McLay & Suzanne Kendrick: Stalwart Advocates of the Freefall Education – I cannot acknowledge you both enough for your contribution.

To Glenn Williams & Azita Moradi: To one of the most inspirational couples I know – thank you for your love and support.

To the Te Tai Whanau (Family): Thank you for accepting me unconditionally

To Matt Church: Thank you for the priceless gift of being seen and heard for the first time in my life.

To Lisa Messenger: Thanks for believing in this book in the early stages of its development.

To Lucinda Beacham: Thank you for persevering with knowing this book had what it took to be published one day.

To David Ord: Ghost writer extraordinaire, your gift of writing is second to none, and I will write all future books with you. Your contribution and partnership have been divinely orchestrated.

To my many mentors (you know who you are): Thank you for believing in me even before I knew.

To my friends: Thanks for believing in me, supporting me, and loving me!

To the many friends who have come in and out of my life: Thank you for playing a part in my evolution.

Ultimately to Spirit: Where were you when I needed you? You were the one carrying me. Thank you for always being there even when I never knew you were!

Contents

PART II
my life apprenticeship

introduction

The approach to transformation described in *Freefall* has helped people who have sought change for years to finally upgrade their lives to a degree that exceeds their hopes and dreams.

Using the *Freefall* approach, individuals at last quit seeking and "trying to get there," at last enjoying a rewarding and meaningful life.

The *Freefall* approach works by enabling people to alter their perception of their past, which frees them to live authentically in the present. They then gain the power to design their future in such a way as to fulfill their unique legacy.

Sally Anderson is one of Australasia's foremost thinkers in sustainable transformation. As a truly cutting edge leadership coach, inspirational female speaker, seminar leader, and master coach trainer, she has inspired thousands who have felt disempowered in their personal and professional lives, enabling them to achieve outstanding sustainable results. Through her dedication to the advancement of human performance, Sally Anderson is a pioneer in the field of human consciousness. With her trademark passion and stalwart commitment, she is devoted to sharing her wealth of knowledge, spreading her message to an ever-increasing audience by taking the mystery out of achieving sustainable results.

As a foundation for her revolutionary approach, Sally has twenty years of corporate experience, latterly as Program Director for one of the world's leading Fortune 500 Companies. Not only is she an expert in her field, but she also brings to the table her personal story of triumph over one of the worst crimes ever reported in New Zealand, as profiled in the New Zealand television program *60 Minutes*. Her unique personal perspective, traumatic history, and mastery as a transformational coach provide her with a rare combination of talents that inform not only our personal lives but also the business world.

Sally is one of the pre-eminent speakers and transformation coaches we have seen in our time, and her courageously candid message, practical strategies, and fresh ideas invite us to examine, reassess, and reframe our life events so we might realize the greatness that exists within us.

In both the personal and professional arenas, Sally helps people overcome the greatest obstacle to their success—*themselves*. Given that she has overcome obstacles most would deem insurmountable, Sally's life reads like a great fictional epic in which the heroine overcomes all odds, then turns around to empower others to do the same.

No one knows better than Sally Anderson that we each have the power to create a triumphant ending for our own story.

noche oscura

The dark night of the soul ... can happen to anyone. I believe that in some ways it happens to everyone. Yet it is much more significant than simple misfortune. It is a deep transformation, a movement toward indescribable freedom and joy. And in truth it doesn't always have to be unpleasant!

... The dark night is a profoundly good thing. It is an ongoing spiritual process in which we are liberated from attachments and compulsions and empowered to live and love more freely. Sometimes this letting go of old ways is painful, occasionally even devastating. But this is not why the night is called "dark". The darkness of the night implies nothing sinister, only that the liberation takes place in hidden ways, beneath our knowledge and understanding. It happens mysteriously, in secret, and beyond our conscious control. For that reason it can be disturbing or even scary, but in the end it always works to our benefit.

More than anything, I think the dark night of the soul gives meaning to life.

... The meaning revealed in the dark night is beyond understanding.

Gerald G. May, MD, *The Dark Night of the Soul – A Psychiatrist Explores the Connection Between Darkness and Spiritual Growth.* Harper San Francisco, 2004

3

ending the
never-ending
search

Chapter 1

is your life
in default?

Are you living your life by *design* or by *default?*

By "default," I mean the disempowered way so many of us learned to think and feel about ourselves based on the culture, beliefs, and values adopted from our teachers, peers, and the family in which we grew up.

Most of us are disassociated from the emotional pain the default inflicts and how it governs our lives. I'm not talking about the pain that comes from an injury, sickness, or the sadness that accompanies a divorce or the passing of a person we love, but about the pain deep inside each of us that drives our less than beneficial behavior, restricting our enjoyment of life and limiting our potential

It's the heaviness, the weariness of spirit, and the cry of the heart for fulfillment that I'm speaking of.

We live in a world where most people have no idea they are living from a default identity and no idea they are unconscious of who they really are. They don't realize there's an entirely different person at their core than the person they think they are.

I choose not to operate from my default perspective because it doesn't empower me. I don't believe it's anything like our true nature. As a matter of fact, I believe our default identity only has the existence *we give it,* because it's nothing more than a construct in our head. It's a subhuman way of existing that has nothing to do with living as a real human being whose fundamental nature is unconditionally loving.

When we operate from our default identity, we are largely cut off from our loving essence. I believe it's possible not only to access our essence but to live from it on a continual basis.

I learned through extreme circumstances how even the most degrading of human behavior in which terrible atrocities are perpetrated against us doesn't have the final say. Devastating though such atrocities may be at the time, they have no abiding reality and therefore no ultimate ability to define us because they don't originate in our essence. There's something much more enduring and ultimately far more powerful than the worst humans can do when they behave in ways that are completely foreign to their true nature.

In this I speak as an authority. Indeed, I am my *own* authority because I have plunged to the depths of degradation and found this place to have no substance. I *know* our essential nature is unconditional love. Intrigued? Read on.

When we live in our default identity, love is always conditional. That's because this lower level of consciousness is based on fear. Fear has to do with *ego*, which someone has rightly dubbed Edging God Out. In contrast, high-level consciousness is connected to Source, which is love. This Source is our true being. When we function from our true being, we experience nothing but love. We become a person who is so different from anything we have ever known ourselves to be that we are all but unrecognizable.

There are always two contexts for everything—one that's empowered, and one that's disempowered. The default that I'm speaking of is a *disempowered* context. I'm referring to a way of approaching life learned in the past, but that no longer serves us. I have had the privilege of coaching many professionals throughout my career, and most coaches don't know about their own default, which renders them unable to recognize when their clients are in default. Is it any wonder we continue to have so many disempowered people in spite of all the counseling and coaching that has arisen in modern times? Imagine if coaches, counselors, psychiatrists, social workers—anyone who has the privilege of enhancing the human condition—were armed with insight into the default and how it disempowers, in addition to what they already know. We would end our oscillation between feeling empowered and disempowered. At last able to sustain an empowered state, we would live up to our potential.

what real transformation is

Following a workshop in which I had asserted that our lives can be unrecognizably transformed, an extremely intelligent man in his mid forties asked me, "How can we be unrecognizably transformed? If we were unrecognizably transformed, we wouldn't recognize it."

When I speak about unrecognizable transformation, I'm saying we die at our default level of identity. This isn't an intellectual concept, it's an experiential occurrence. It's akin to the metamorphosis a caterpillar goes through when it becomes first a chrysalis and then a butterfly. A single life flows through the different stages of its existence, but each stage is a radically different experience from what the caterpillar originally knew itself to be. So it is with us. We're the same person and yet totally different.

Metamorphosis involves a death of sorts. The transformation of the caterpillar into a chrysalis symbolizes the death we each have to go through in order to become free of our default identity, while the birth of the butterfly from the chrysalis symbolizes our emergence into an entirely new quality of consciousness.

Transformation is fundamentally different from self-improvement. Later in the book I'll illustrate the difference from my own life. I was a walking trigger, but being triggered was causing me so much pain that I felt like I was dying inside. Still, I imagined that if I could just apply all the information I was receiving from the countless courses I took, books I read, and audio programs I listened to, I would become free of pain. However, no matter how many avenues I tried, I was unable to sustain most of the changes I attempted to make.

I told myself that if I believed in the teachings of my latest spiritual teacher, I would be a changed person. If I applied a certain set of principles, I would be different. If I followed a particular spiritual or religious path, I would be transformed. Yet after years of courses, I wasn't transformed. I was still a walking trigger.

conformity is the opposite of presence

There's a widespread notion that unless we follow a certain path, we can't access the holy grail of consciousness of our true being. This is a dangerous belief because it leads to control and conformity, which are the antithesis of becoming fully aware of and present in our moment-by-moment existence.

People imagine that an individual who is conscious of their true self and living from their authentic being should act in a certain way, instead of recognizing that consciousness can be expressed in a myriad of forms. Many of us feel pressured to fall in line with this expectation of what a conscious life is supposed to look like. If we don't conform, we feel we aren't "spiritual." But there is no "should" or "ought" to authentic spirituality because such rules violate the essence of what it is to be *real,* which is the hallmark of spirituality.

To be conscious, and therefore free to be who we really are instead of being driven by past hurt, isn't to hold a set of concepts of how a free person acts: A conscious person doesn't smoke, they eat a certain way, they dress a certain way, they use certain words when they talk. None of this has anything to do with consciousness. It's just a mask, a pretense of spirituality.

Consciousness isn't a cookie cutter culture in which one shape fits all. What might work for you might not work for me. There are many, many ways of experiencing authenticity. The right to determine the course of our life is ours and ours alone. If we choose to adopt a behavior that doesn't serve us, such as smoking, that's our right as a free person. For this reason, we pay no attention to the person who challenges: "How can you possibly be spiritual and smoke?" or "How can you possibly be spiritual and drink?"

While we can't be conscious and willingly harm others, this doesn't mean we live our life trying to fit into the picture people create of what a conscious person ought to act like. If an individual manifests a degree of default behavior alongside their emerging consciousness, the spiritual person manages the default behavior as something separate from the individual's essential being. It's crucial not to collapse the behavior into who we imagine someone is.

Spirituality—consciousness of our authentic being—is just *embracing what is.* A transformed existence is one in which we embrace freedom moment-by-moment experientially as the free flow of life itself, which is fundamentally different from abiding by a set of mental concepts. In other words, to be spiritual means we embrace the whole of our being, showing up in all of our magnificence.

But if it were this easy, surely everybody would be experiencing it wouldn't they?

Considering the number of people who are searching for fulfillment and not finding it, it would seem it must be a secret only a token number grasp. However, I discovered that nothing could be further from the truth. Everybody *can* experience a wonderful life in which they don't hurt anymore.

The tendency to complicate what it means to be spiritual is rooted in our need to avoid actually *being* spiritual, which I repeat is just to be real and experience presence in each and every situation. We like to keep things complicated because our default identity can't grasp being present with a person or a particular set of circumstances and allowing consciousness to guide us from moment to moment. In order to continue in our confusion, in which (as we shall see) we have an investment, we embrace concepts of what spirituality is "supposed" to be instead of simply being conscious.

To finally arrive at experiencing the answers to life as very straightforward would eradicate the need for the vicious cycle of self-improvement so many of us engage in. Instead of life being a struggle to improve ourselves, it would become a spontaneous unfolding of each individual's potential, a flourishing of who each of us is in our uniqueness.

To embrace our unique expression of consciousness means we're going to dress differently, speak differently, behave differently, and choose a path in life that will be different from anyone else's path.

Why would our path be different from everyone else's? Because when we're true to ourselves, we live from our Source, which is infinite in its diversity. Just look at the world of nature or at the vast array of galaxies. It's obvious Spirit delights in pouring forth a torrent of variety.

why we can't make the teaching work

As long as I was doing things the precise way a particular methodology advocated, my life oscillated between moments of happiness and times of extreme misery. I enjoyed some semblance of happiness, but it lasted only as long as I applied the method—and even then it worked only partially, just enough to keep me going back for more teaching and training.

Why couldn't I make the teaching work? Because I was trying to create for myself a reality that wasn't possible. A person who is coming from their default identity simply can't live a transformed life. It's as impossible as it is for a caterpillar or a chrysalis to fly.

Having said this, let me reassert that I believe in radical transformation, to the point that we become unrecognizable from our default perspective. Hence, whenever people tell me (which they do often), "It's not possible to be that transformed," I respond, "That's a belief. If you believe you can be transformed, you can. But if you believe you can't, you can't."

Such a belief is part of our default identity, a product of the way we've grown up. It has nothing to do with our authentic self. By "authentic," I mean the person we are in our essence, the person we were before we learned that to be real wasn't acceptable. We have all adopted a pseudo identity in conformity to or in rebellion against what we believed those who were significant in our life expected of us.

In our essential being, we have always been unconditional love. This is what we have the potential to become in every dimension of our everyday life. However, even though we were born unconditionally loving and this continues to be our core state, in our default self-understanding we are completely unconscious of unconditional love. This is because all we have ever experienced is love that's conditional. Hence when unconditional love begins to arise in us, it can feel strange and even frightening. We're afraid to allow such a powerful love to infiltrate the persona we exude because it would mean the collapse of our default identity, which is the only sense of "self" with which we are familiar.

I want to emphasize that although unconditional love feels strange at first, we actually yearn for it. Because we were born unconditionally loving but have forgotten what it feels like, it's a case of remembering.

Because it's so important to grasp the difference between our authentic being and our default identity, let me repeat what I said earlier: that when someone says it isn't possible for us to be transformed to the point we are unrecognizable, this is actually accurate from the perspective of our default identity. This is why the *death* of who we have known ourselves to be is essential if we are to experience transformation.

transformation requires a death

Most self-development programs I know of teach people how to manage their different states, not how to die altogether to their default identity.

A high percentage of spiritual paths also teach we can only be empowered if we believe in something other than ourselves. Though there are spiritual paths that talk about looking within, even these tend to point to a reality other than who we are at this moment. This is because at the core of these teachings is the idea there is an ultimately "real" reality that's the place we will finally arrive if we faithfully follow their program.

The promise is that it's going to be better than where we are right now. We're assured that if we rely on spirit—either an external spirit or what many refer to as the "spirit within"—in the way a particular teacher defines spirit, we'll eventually "arrive."

If you look at all the people who follow a teacher, they are being offered an empowered state based on believing in this particular teacher's path. If they don't believe the teacher's way, they're told they won't experience this empowered state. It's a vicious cycle, keeping an oscillation between being empowered and disempowered going interminably.

In this sense, it's an addiction. With alcoholism, drugs, gambling, sexual addiction—in fact, any addiction—we're looking to something external to make a difference in our life. Even when we talk about our Higher Power, many of us are looking to something other than who *we* are *right now* in ourselves. As long as we believe that "one day," if we follow certain principles and believe certain concepts, things will be better, we will oscillate between functionality and dysfunction.

I never found any of these paths sustainable because while they facilitate a measure of improvement, they keep the paradigm of our default identity in place, which is disempowering. How can we experience transformation of the dysfunctional aspects of our life when we operate from our default identity, which by its very nature is incapable of undergoing a metamorphosis?

Our default identity prefers self-improvement, which is why everyone is looking for an empowered state through some technique or other. Most of us are unwilling to pay the price of actually experiencing an empowered state since it requires the death of the person we believe ourselves to be. Because this is a frightening experience for an ego-based identity, we prefer to seek transformation from some source outside of ourselves. But to really change, we have to let go of self-improvement, let go of trying to fix ourselves, and quite simply die to who we think we are.

Let me say this again because it's pivotal. The conscious journey isn't about becoming a better person. It's about dying to the person we have believed ourselves to be and waking up to who we really are in our essence. Unless we are prepared to die to everything we have known ourselves to be, we will forever oscillate between functional and dysfunctional behavior.

When I look back now, I realize that the systems I studied and tried so hard to make work actually kept in place the paradigm of oscillation between being empowered one minute and disempowered the next. They enabled me to avoid having to be responsible for my own emotional and mental state, and consequently I continued to seek a change of circumstances to make me feel better.

In contrast, when we die at the level of our default identity, it's the end of all oscillation. Can you imagine actually experiencing the end of all oscillation? I'm talking about the ability to sustain an empowered state.

To illustrate, let me share a story I read some years ago. A hunter goes into a jungle and captures a parrot. Crossing to the other side of the jungle, he puts the parrot in a cage. The parrot isn't stupid. It knows that if it's going to escape the cage, it needs to enrol the hunter to teach it to speak English so they can communicate.

This done, the parrot says to the hunter, "You have been so nice to me, would you do me a favor? Go to the other side of the jungle, find my best friend, and tell him that I love being in my cage and there's no need for concern."

The hunter feels this is the least he can do, so he finds the parrot's best friend and delivers the message. The parrot's best friend promptly drops dead and the hunter is terribly confused.

When the hunter reports what happened to the parrot in the cage, this parrot also drops dead. Now the hunter is doubly confused. He puts his hand in the cage, picks up the parrot, and tosses it onto a garbage heap. Whereupon the parrot flies up into a tree.

The hunter says to the parrot, "You tricked me."

To which the parrot responds, "My friend was sending me a powerful message."

Asks the hunter, "What was the message?"

Says the parrot, "That I must die in the cage as I know it to find the freedom to fly."

When we die at our default level of identity, transformation becomes sustainable. We can then increasingly choose to live from our true identity, which is empowering. It's empowering because it's grounded in our infinite Source.

a moment-by-moment choice

If we are prepared to surrender our default identity so we can evolve to our full magnitude, our potential is tremendous.

However, if we are interested in evolving consciously toward our potential, many variations of the death process are required to bring us to new levels. Transcending our egoic identity isn't just a one-time individual experience. We are involved in nothing less than the transformation of the human species.

Once we have this framework of understanding, it's a moment-by-moment choice to live in awareness. So many of us are either out in the future creating a world that's not yet here or we are in the past regretting and resenting, none of which has anything to do with our real self. I'm not offering people a world in which, in a future-based paradigm, life will be better. I teach people to take responsibility moment by moment for their state of being right now.

I'm talking about shifting into an entirely different state based on our authentic feeling self. For this reason it's critical to make the shift in what we are committed to experientially, in contrast to analytically and intellectually. If we only get it at a head level, we don't integrate it—and we have to integrate it if we're ever to sustain it. We simply can't do this at a mental level.

For instance, a person tells themselves: "I hate being an alcoholic. I so want my life to be different. I just can't stand being this way."

My response is, "You might say you hate it at a conceptual level. But at a feeling level, you don't hate it, you love it. If you really hated it you wouldn't take another sip." That which we feed reveals what we are really committed to.

Each moment of each day, we get to choose which state we wish to live in based on how it makes us feel. The trouble is, most of us really don't know what we are committed to because we are dissociated from our feelings, which means we can't make wise choices.

Having said this, it's important to point out that most professions that deal with trauma address what they call a person's "feelings," but they are generally dealing with our default reactive *emotions,* not the true feelings of the heart.

Sometimes people who don't recognize the distinction between default emotions and the true feelings of the heart say to me, "But Sally, you are denying me my feelings."

I respond, "Only your default emotions. Feelings are different. Look at a rose and experience the full wonder of its beauty. Enjoy to the hilt the love of a partner. Be filled with joy by the cooing of a newborn baby. Thrill to the excitement of a great adventure. Bask in a compliment from a stranger." All of these invite the loving center of our being to blossom. They evoke feelings that manifest who we really are—feelings that are empowering.

When we're unaware, we don't delineate between the default-based emotions of our disempowered state and the power-based feelings of our empowered state. Instead we react to life. By "react," I mean that when something happens, the mind goes through four phases: we first recognize, next evaluate, then experience a sensation, and are subsequently triggered into reaction. This reaction usually happens in a heartbeat and is always disempowering.

The irony is that when we are aware, our default-based emotion becomes the access point for collapsing past and future mental projections and shifting to awareness of the present moment. In other words, emotional reactions and the pain they cause are what ultimately train us to live in the now.

To help clients feel, I request they produce a photo of themselves between the ages of three and five. I encourage them to look at this photo and *re-presence* themselves to who they were before they shut down.

I witnessed how powerful this simple exercise can be from the case of a CEO who I asked to reconnect with a photo of himself as a little boy aged four. This was a hard-nosed, unemotional, extremely cynical businessman who thought it was ridiculous that we were entertaining this process. Nevertheless, when he pondered the photo of himself, he burst into tears. He realized what a huge betrayal his life had been of who he really was. About three-quarters of my clients have a similar reaction.

Once we realize that our true being isn't the same as our default identity, we no longer feed this false identity because we realize it doesn't serve us anymore.

Having said this, I want to emphasize that, as destructive as it is, our default identity is actually a safety mechanism that needs to be acknowledged for its role in having protected us during the years we were unaware of our true being. I will illustrate how this worked in my own life in due course. In the meantime, it's important to recognize that at each stage of our journey, we were doing the best we could, for which our default identity was responsible.

If everybody came from their true being instead of their default identity, we would have a transformed world in which unconditional love is the mode of being in every aspect of life. The only reason it doesn't happen is because too few of us believe it's possible and even fewer of us are taking a stand for it.

Chapter 2

the seeker who cannot find

At an introductory evening to one of my seminars, I shared with my audience that I had invested hundreds of thousands of dollars in working on myself.

Over a twenty-year period, while my peers were dating, getting married, raising children, buying houses, and having a so-called "normal" existence, I went from one self-improvement course to another in search of some semblance of sanity because I had such a persistent urge to end my life. I was literally an addicted course junkie!

A seventy-five-year-old woman in the audience challenged: "I'm just like you. I've read the books, listened to the audio programs, and done all the courses. What makes you think your teaching is any different?"

I have observed that people are generally receptacles when they attend a lecture or take a course. They generally don't want to have to change *themselves,* they want someone to change them. If you listen closely, you can hear this in the language of the woman who quizzed me about my approach. She was saying in effect, "What are *you* going to do for me all the others I listened to couldn't?"

In response, I invited her to take a closer look at what was actually going on in her search. "Why, all these years," I probed, "have you continued to go to seminars that have cost you a lot of time and money, and tolerate not getting the transformation you want?"

She replied, "What choice did I have?"

I said, "You could decide you won't stand for it any longer."

She looked mystified, so I explained: "It's a matter of no longer tolerating not getting the transformation you've sought all your life. I'd like you to entertain the possibility that, like myself, you've been 'seeking' all these years because until now you haven't really wanted to commit to the changed life you say you want. If you had, you would be transformed by now!"

While we may appear enthusiastic about transformation, most of the time our actions show we are in fact more committed to keeping in place our belief that it's not possible to be transformed.

Let me be clear what I mean. I'm saying that nobody in their right mind would pay time and time again to attend something that doesn't actually change them unless *not* changing were what they were *really* committed to.

why transformation eludes us

Saying we want transformation but maintaining the status quo seems to be the norm for most of us who seek to change ourselves.

In fact, in my experience a high percentage of self-improvement programs really don't expect dramatic transformation to happen in the lives of people who take the program. They are designed to allow us to circumvent instantaneous change by advocating a philosophy that says "life will be better *when...*"

In contrast to this, it's vital to understand that "this is it." There is nowhere else to go, nowhere to "get to."

From what I observe, the majority of us live in a world where this *isn't* "it" yet. We think there's somewhere else to get to. In fact, we're wired to focus on a future-based world because we're dissatisfied with our current world. We want to get somewhere other than where we are right now, imagining that when we get there it will be better than where we are at present. Clients continually say to me, "I'm getting there." But where is this place called "there?"

I ask a client, "How's it going?"

Back comes the response, "I'm getting there."

When they tell me they're "getting there," I recognize the dissatisfaction that's at the core of trying to live in this future place called "there." To help them get a clear picture of it for themselves, I ask, "Where for you is this place called 'there?'"

Then, because they are a client, they remember what I teach, which is that we can only ever be in the here and now. "Oh, I know, I know." They get it from a head point of view but not in their heart. If they actually knew it experientially instead of just analytically, they wouldn't be striving to reach a destination at which they'll never arrive.

Once we understand that "this is it," we relax and live knowing we've already arrived. In fact, we've never not been exactly where we tell ourselves we long to be.

Let me hasten to add that to embrace the statement "this is it" doesn't mean having no goals, dreams, or aspirations. It means focusing on the *now* moment, the twenty-four hours we have today. So the question is: Who am I going to be on *this* day, right now? Not who do I hope to be tomorrow or the next day, but who am I at *this* moment?

To understand that "this is it" is the essence of satisfaction. The realization there *truly* is nowhere to "get to" can be quite cathartic!

the never-ending search

This brings us back to the question I asked the woman in my audience: Why do we take a course, go on a retreat, read a book, listen to audio programs, invest a great deal of money in coaching or counseling, yet seem okay with the fact we aren't fundamentally and forever changed?

I've been through far more personal development programs than most. In one way or another, the majority of the programs I engaged in contributed to my growth. Yet somehow I failed to cross the line into really coming "home" to myself in the way I longed to do.

Countless people told me of a speaker I just had to hear, a book I simply must read, or a coach who was "dynamite." As desperate as I was, I tried them all. Whenever I went to hear a speaker, participated in a retreat, or took a course, I experienced a shot of euphoria. In fact, I felt great for the duration of the self-improvement event I was attending. At times, I even caught a vision of who I could be. I became profoundly aware that the person I believed myself to be wasn't really who I was. But though this glimpse of my real self was inspiring for a while, the changes I made were of only limited effectiveness and were never sustainable. When I resumed my everyday routine, it was only to find that within a short time I had been sucked back into the same old, same old.

I doubt my experience of the self-help programs I engaged in is unique to me. So let me ask you: Have you ever experienced what I'm talking about?

a global phenomenon

Hoping for transformation in the future isn't just a problem we experience individually. It's a global phenomenon.

We have an entire planet of people who say they want transformation of one kind or another. They want to experience change in their personal lives, their relationships, and their work environment. They want transformation of the political and economic systems. And they want our planet to be transformed into a peaceful world in which wars cease, violent crime is no more, and we don't pollute our air, soil, and water.

If all of us who say we want transformation really did want it, our lives and our world would be transformed. The reality is that we are more committed to the benefits we're receiving from our current state than we are to transformation.

We can see this so clearly in the commercial world. For instance, take the weight loss industry, which is a billion dollar business. Think of how many people you know who have tried to lose weight again and again yet never sustained the loss. I came to realize that what we are *truly* committed to shows in the results we get. Globally, what we are getting is people who can't sustain weight loss, which shows that *telling* themselves they want to lose weight is what they are committed to, not to actually achieving their ideal weight. If the legion of people who try to lose weight really wanted transformation, we would have millions of people who are sustaining weight loss.

Another multi-billion dollar business, the tobacco industry, knows that large numbers of people believe they want to quit smoking for the sake of their health. But the industry is savvy enough to recognize that most smokers are not *actually* committed to their health above all else or they would never take another puff. Though people say they've been trying to quit forever, in reality they're far more interested in sedating their anxiety, which a cigarette does almost instantly since nicotine is a highly effective drug. Because the tobacco industry knows that people value calming their anxiety above improving their health, it's no problem for them to print on cigarette packets a government warning that the Surgeon General of the United States has determined tobacco is injurious to a person's health. They know people are less committed to wellness than to easing their emotional pain.

One more example will suffice: the pharmaceutical industry. Certain aspects of this industry have no real commitment to eradicating depression, post-traumatic stress disorder, bipolar disease, ADHD, Asperger's, autism, suicidal tendencies, and the like, because the financial feedback loop is too lucrative.

What's true of the pharmaceutical industry is also true of many who seek treatment. They turn again and again to pharmaceuticals and imagine they are committed to wellness. What we are really committed to can be seen by looking at the results we get. I was a classic example. I was overweight for eighteen years, smoked like a chimney, used drugs to pacify myself, and indulged in a host of dysfunctional behaviors.

From talking with countless people who have been on the path to consciousness for a long time like myself, it's my assessment that less than ten percent of all who embark on the various paths to personal transformation emerge from their experience transformed.

disempowered by what we tolerate

It's ludicrous to do the same thing over and over and expect different results, yet almost the entire planet is doing it. This is because humans as a species have a way of tolerating a great deal. When I use the word "tolerate," I'm not referring to our capacity to handle times of difficulty or adversity. I'm referring to our acceptance of things that disempower us on a daily basis.

I recommend that clients identify and write down what they tolerate in their lives. It's quite an alarming exercise for most because they have never allowed themselves to tune into the undercurrent that operates in their subconscious. Doing this exercise is a powerful way of bringing this undercurrent into our awareness. When people actually write down what they tolerate, they are usually shocked by how many areas of their life are affected by undercurrents that work against what they say they want for themselves.

Life lived in the tow of these undercurrents is what I call our "default identity." The undercurrents keep us from being—and often even recognizing—who we *really* are.

Most of us tolerate attitudes that work against us both in ourselves and in others. We tolerate things at an organizational level and in our business life. We especially seem to tolerate behavior that doesn't benefit us in our home environment and relationships with individuals like our siblings, parents, or children. And, of course, we tolerate a great deal in ourselves, ranging from something as simple as always being late, to putting up with a faulty door handle on a bathroom cabinet that's been irritating us for months.

When we shed light on everything we tolerate, we become present to the undercurrents we operate "over the top of" every single day of our lives.

To help clients become aware of the undercurrents that rule them, I pose the question: "What would your life look like if you didn't tolerate anything?"

The typical response is: "That's not possible."

A life in which we don't tolerate anything of a disempowering nature is not only possible, it's a very different kind of life. For one thing, there's no longer anything to complain about. When you consider how many times in a day we complain about our circumstances, are mad at ourselves because we didn't do something that was important, don't put something in its proper place so we can find it again, or rant about the traffic making us late because we didn't allow enough time—things we could easily do something about—you realize we siphon off a tremendous amount of potentially creative energy as useless negativity that changes nothing.

Once we shed light on something, it no longer "has" us. We're now free to choose whether we wish to continue a particular behavior or drop it. But until we commit to a choice, we're in its power instead of our own.

When we live predominantly at a lower level of consciousness, we are only able to evolve through adversity. Despite the consciousness we've achieved as a species, we still seem to learn predominantly only through adversity. Given our present state, spirit uses adversity to wake us up because we wouldn't choose of our own accord to wake up. Only through adversity are we finally forced to change our thinking and alter our emotional state. Only when we *hurt* enough do we at last become committed.

At this level of consciousness, adversity is our apprenticeship. However, we can evolve beyond the need to manifest adversity in order to learn. When we do, we will experience a world in which nobody hurts anymore. In such a world, we'll no longer need to manifest adversity.

For me this isn't a highfalutin concept but a potential reality. The only reason it hasn't happened yet is because we just aren't choosing it. But the point is, we can! And I believe we will.

In fact, I believe you and I can choose it *this very day*.

Chapter 3

w h y   i   d o n ' t   b e l i e v e
i n   d e p r e s s i o n

In my seminars, I encounter people who have been seeing a practitioner in one of the helping professions for years. It may be a psychotherapist, counselor, social worker, life coach, priest, psychiatrist, or medical doctor who prescribes medication for depression.

Though countless people seek professional help, read books, and go on courses in an attempt to feel happier, the vast amount of psychological understanding available today hasn't altered the fact that depression is rife on every continent and people are topping themselves all over the planet.

I'm convinced it doesn't have to be this way. I will also share with you that if you like going to a counselor or coach for an extended period of time, in excess of twelve months, you may have difficulty "being with" what I state here, for I do not believe in creating a dependency with those we seek to enlighten.

When an individual labels themselves as "depressed" because of overwhelming default feelings that disempower them, why does society compound the situation with a double cocktail of *disassociation*? Our circumstances can catapult us into a disassociated state, which is one thing. But to then legalize the issuing of drugs to numb an individual to a level of complete disassociation is another. Where I ask is the logic in this?

the ludicrousness cycle

Someone in a seminar challenged me that what I was teaching wasn't working. This woman had numerous ailments and complained continually. I asked, "Would you agree that you take almost no action?"

"That's true," she admitted. She then went on to bemoan the fact she was hindered by the illnesses she suffered and consequently was depressed.

I explained, "If you take little or no action and therefore don't get the results you want, it's not at all surprising you would spiral down into what you would term a 'depressed state.' If we take no action or the same action as we always take, it will inevitably lead to a feeling of hopelessness."

I pointed out to this woman that if she wanted to experience a break in the cycle, she needed to identify the places in which she was abdicating her responsibility. Needless to say, she became confused. How convenient! Confusion is humanity's biggest relinquishment bucket. We don't want to own that the area of our life in which we abdicate responsibility is part of what we want to keep in place so we don't have to be responsible.

Because this woman was unwilling to examine where she was relinquishing responsibility, she manifested illnesses, then coddled them. Of course, her ailments enabled her to make the *teaching* "wrong." To her, they were proof it "didn't work," when it was *she* who wasn't "working." Not present to the costs of being a victim, she was unaware that *she* was the cause of her dysfunction, and she therefore felt powerless to change her situation. In due course, I asked her to leave the program. "Don't pay me money if you're unwilling to be responsible," I told her, "especially when you know what you're doing."

There are enough professionals in the world who dissect our story and have us pay money for the privilege. I have no wish to add to them. Imagine paying a professional to keep our story going! I believe this is ludicrous. After people have already been telling their story year after year, I'm not about to allow them to pay me to talk about the same story on a different channel.

We are the one who created the story, and it's only kept alive because *we keep feeding it.*

It isn't standard practice to call someone to account concerning their depressed state, but I do exactly this. I don't challenge the person's validity as an individual, of course, but I do challenge their thinking. When I do so, I have observed again and again that years of depression evaporate as a result of a simple shift within the person.

the roots of depression

Depression isn't a cause of someone's misery, it's a symptom. I'm interested in what's causing the depression.

I don't believe in this "thing" called depression, as if it's something that just takes us over like an alien force. I believe that when we label ourselves depressed, we do so because we get to abdicate responsibility for our well-being. Buying into the man-made construct called depression lets us off the hook from having to show up in our life for the magnificent person we really are. If we're depressed, how can we be expected to do something meaningful?

I gave a presentation to 250 psychiatrists in Queenstown, New Zealand, in which I pointed out that when a psychiatrist is in the presence of a client who's suicidal, it's my understanding that their standard practice is to deal with the symptom called suicide. It seems to me that the psychiatric industry is fearful when in the presence of a person who's suicidal. I, on the other hand, believe it to be the responsibility of the practitioner to remove our own transference of fear and, instead of backing off, go right into the thick of the symptom all the way to the root.

When I'm in the presence of someone who is suicidal, the first thing I say to them is, "Great!"

Are you surprised by my response? The individual certainly is. However, I find that such a response, because I really *mean* it, is a state-shifter.

Let me warn you that if you are a practitioner and you don't really believe it's great that the person has reached this point in their journey, taking this approach can backfire. I tell the person that where they have arrived is "great" because I believe they are at a juncture where there's actually a possibility for a change of direction.

I'm not fearful of the person who is suicidal because, as I'll in due course relate, having experienced an eighteen-year suicidal conversation myself, I understand the desire to kill oneself better than most. For a person to say they are suicidal is the ultimate cry for attention. I speak from experience when I call someone who says they are suicidal to account. I'm always amazed at their reaction when I respond to their announcement that they are going to end their life, "Great!" In every instance, they laugh. Hmm. One minute they declare they are going to commit suicide, then the next they are laughing. Extraordinary! Used wisely, laughter can be a powerful state shifter.

After I've congratulated the person for arriving at this moment in their life, I ask them point blank, "So, when are you going to do it? On what day and at what time?" Their reaction is to be dumbfounded. Why such a reaction? Because I'm the first person the suicidal individual has ever encountered who *refuses to enroll myself in their drama.*

To say we're suicidal is the most powerful way any of us has to enroll those around us in our drama as a "victim." If someone tells you, "I'm suicidal," they have your full attention.

When I ask a suicidal person for the specific time they plan to kill themselves, they ask with astonishment, "What do you mean?"

My response is, "What do you think I mean? If you were really serious about suicide, you would have done it by now."

When I call someone who's suicidal or depressed to account like this, they go into a state of confusion. I convey to the person that I'm not interested in simply stopping them topping themselves or helping them keep going in their depressed state. I'm interested in them discovering their innate power, which will enable them to free themselves from their suicidal thinking and depression.

At this point, I facilitate a conversation that reveals to the person what they get out of being suicidal or depressed. I want them to see what they are getting out of it in contrast to what it's costing them. Once a person understands not only what their behavior is costing them, but also what they are getting out of it, they are aware of what's really going on. Now they have a choice. If they are willing to be present to what their condition is costing them, they move to a different state of mind in a heartbeat.

The transformation of any dysfunctional behavior is a function of making the individual aware of what in them is running the show. This is why I'm a causal coach instead of a symptomatic coach. Once you present someone with the cause, they can take their power back. From my observation, a high percentage of practitioners are so swayed by the symptoms that they aren't listening for the cause. They are too busy psychoanalyzing the symptoms instead of unearthing what's causing the dysfunction. In this way the client becomes increasingly dependent on the professional instead of on themselves.

People are suicidal because they know *something* in them has to die. In this they are absolutely correct. Something does indeed need to die! But it's not the individual that needs to die, it's the illusion they've bought into about themselves all their life—their default identity.

dealing with a potential suicide

When someone goes to a doctor, a psychiatrist, or a counselor, they usually talk about all their symptoms while trying their hardest to avoid the axis point that's causing their condition.

In fact, because they are attached to keeping their victim status in place, they are likely to become extremely defensive if their thinking is challenged. Suggest that their suicidal thoughts or depression are symptoms of a victim mentality, and they will see you as the devil incarnate! I have had people rear up at me, demanding angrily and loudly: "Who the hell do you think you are? What do you know about all the suffering I'm having to go through?"

If someone is attacking me, from my point of view as an intuitive causal coach, it's pure gold. Their language and emotional state tell me everything I need to know to help shine the light of awareness on what's really going on beneath the individual's suicidal and depressed symptoms.

How many practitioners would view such an attack as gold? It's too easy to freak out in the face of such an attack. The reason people can get away with this behavior is that practitioners allow it. The reason I don't freak out is that I know the abuse has nothing to do with me. It may be aimed at me, but I simply represent all the people who have hurt the individual in the past—the people who were the source of the individual's pain. When there's no reaction on the part of the practitioner, such defensive behavior loses all its power because it can't thrive when it isn't being fueled.

In a therapeutic setting, for the client to say they are suicidal is a kind of power play between the practitioner and the individual. The practitioner needs to be clear whose court they are playing on. If the professional buys into the individual's game and begins playing on their court, they lose all their power to bring about transformation. A practitioner needs to know that one real conversation that goes to the root of the suicidal person's state can be life-transforming.

It's important for the practitioner to stay calm regardless of the client's state. If the practitioner remains calm, the individual will gradually become calm. If the practitioner becomes reactive, feeding their own fears into the drama of the threat of suicide, they end up intensifying the drama.

Whenever fear is present, we are either feeding something in the future, which clearly hasn't occurred yet, or we are dragging something in from the past. If the practitioner is fearful of what the client might do, the practitioner plays a role in the outcome. In the presence of fear, the odds are that the client has the power, and the practitioner is playing on their court.

If a practitioner is intentional about getting someone out of their suicidal mindset, the practitioner has to totally collapse their own defensive state. Then they can really listen for the source of the individual's pain as well as for their greatness.

Once I've brought the person's victim mentality into the light of day, I listen to them at a level they've never experienced before in their life. They've never been in the presence of someone who listens to their greatness beneath their façade of victimhood, or they wouldn't be in the state they're in. To be listened to in this way is one of the most healing experiences a person can have.

Going to the brink of suicide can prove to be a powerful preparation for a person to enter into the total trust required for freefall. It's precisely how some of the world's most conscious spiritual leaders became the powerhouses they have become. However, if we *stay* in a low state, it's because we're getting something out of it.

When we are experiencing a so-called "high," we are enjoying a high level of excitement. What would happen if we experienced the same level of excitement when we perceive ourselves as "low?"

When we feel low, or life seems to have taken a bad turn, we are operating from a low level of consciousness. This is because we're living in the realm of default-based meaning. We can never have a bad day when we are in our empowered state.

Losing the pseudo power of our default identity equips us to find our real power.

What would your life look like if you never had a bad day or a low moment ever again?

Nothing can be good or bad unless we are making it mean something. There can be *no* angst in life unless we continue to live at the low consciousness of egoic meaning. I'm a true believer in equanimity, which is the ability to remain undisturbed in the face of perceived good or ill fortune. To lead an equanimous life is the ultimate!

I find it interesting that the word depression and recession are so similar. I know that many experience depression or say that they are impacted by a recession, but I do not believe in either depression or a recession. I believe that both depression and recession are a global epidemic of fear, whereby people buy into disempowerment. I know of people who have thrived in business in so-called recessions; and I also know of people who, when called to account, laugh in the presence of a powerful practitioner when the word "depression" is mentioned. All I wish to bring to your attention is the power of language: words create the experience of the world. If you want your experience of the world to shift, change your language. Then it holds no power.

I have a passion to make a fundamental difference to the way counseling and psychotherapy is administered. In this field is goes against practice to share anything of a personal nature. As a transformation agent one has to go toe to toe with a client to access the unprecedented level of authenticity that exists beyond ego. I believe there is another way for people to reclaim their power than to disassociate themselves from that which they created. Drugs are not the answer.

I also believe for a practitioner to facilitate another's default they need to have an integral understanding of their own default identity.

Chapter 4

what do you want for your life?

The standard response people give when I ask them what they want for their life is, "To be happy." When I ask them how they plan to achieve this, it's as if happiness were an elusive state that occurs only on those rare occasions when our circumstances line up in a particularly favorable way.

We're waiting for our life to change and give us this illusory state called happiness, but happiness has nothing to do with our external circumstances changing. In fact, our circumstances have no impact on our happiness either positive or negatively unless we allow them to. This is because to experience happiness is a matter of our moment by moment choices, based on what we say we are committed to.

I have worked with clients who are extremely wealthy, with the kind of lifestyle and every material possession a human being could want, and yet they aren't happy. I have also worked with clients who want what these clients have because they imagine if they had these things, they'd be happy.

The popular belief that when we get the house of our dreams, the boat, the man or woman, and the dog, then we'll be in this state called "happiness," actually keeps us from attaining the happiness we seek. We're looking to the future to fulfill us in the present, which is by definition impossible.

I say to people who have all the trappings of happiness, "Is this *it* for you yet?"

Invariably they respond, "Oh, God, no! I've got the house, the boat, the man or woman, and the dog, but I still need the sports car, a specific piece of

35

artwork or another investment property." As long as we live in a past-future paradigm instead of in this moment right now, we'll always be dissatisfied.

We've been wired since childhood to wait for the circumstances around us to shift before we ourselves shift. But if we want our external world to shift, we must first shift our internal world. In other words, we're waiting for our circumstances to shift our inner state, whereas our inner state needs to shift our external circumstances.

How many books do we need to read before we finally "get it" that our inner reality really does govern our outer reality?

which movie are you playing?

Seeking happiness is an elusive quest because we don't deal in reality, only in *projections*.

Think of it in terms of watching a movie. The projector represents us, or more precisely our inner state. The screen represents our life and circumstances, while the film represents our worldview—our way of thinking.

If we go to a video store, pick out a DVD, place it in the DVD player, and begin watching the movie, we aren't surprised by what shows up on the screen because this is what we chose to watch. Well, our life parallels this. The film we choose to place in our projector, which is our internal state, is exactly what will show up on the screen of life's circumstances. When we aren't disciplined to monitor our internal state, the dissatisfaction and perhaps chaos we experience in our everyday life are simply projections of our internal disarray.

Remember the movie Ten? Though it was all about looks, the fact is that life is less than the wonderful experience it could be when, in any area of our life, we settle for being less than a Ten.

I often ask my clients where they are on a scale of zero to ten in how they feel about their life. Of course, most of us indulge in a lot of wishful thinking around the idea of being a Ten, but the majority are realistic enough to say they are somewhere between a Five and a Ten, with a handful admitting they operate at an even lower level.

To be a Ten is to resonate with life at our highest potential. If we are operating at anything less than a Ten, we resonate with and therefore attract life experiences at that lower level. For example, if we are operating at a Five, it's because we have a Five film playing through our projector, resonating with and attracting Five experiences.

I next ask my clients, "If the difference between a Five and a Ten is five, where does the missing five live—in the past, the present, or the future?"

The client usually responds, "When I get beyond my past, and when I get what I want in the future, then I will be a Ten."

I answer, "Why not just place a Ten film in there right now? It's a simple matter of a choice."

Personally, I choose to be a Ten throughout my entire day. Why? Because having lived much of my life as a Zero, I'm profoundly aware there's nothing like living as a Ten.

So when I go to the local supermarket and the checkout person asks me how I am, I respond, "Absolutely extraordinary!"

The clerk then asks, "What happened?"

I say, "Nothing. I just choose to feel this way."

When I awakened to the fact that all my life I had functioned from a default-based identity that was nothing like my real identity, I realized that living a joyful life is a function of choosing to embrace my true state, not a function of my circumstances shifting. In each moment, I can choose to incarnate the default identity I believed myself to be all those years when I was miserable, or I can choose to be true to who I am at my core.

choosing to be happy

If we aren't happy, it's because we're not choosing to be happy, regardless of our circumstances or the actions of others.

"But don't you realize what I've been through?" a woman said to me one time in a coaching session. "You have no idea what it feels like!" This client had endured several relationships in which she was abused emotionally, sexually, and physically. Three times she had married similar types of men.

In dialogue with my client, she repeatedly made statements such as, "I have had a shit life," "I have had shit dealt to me," "They have laid their shit on me," and "I've still got to deal with their shit because we had a child together." How people talk about their experience of life speaks volumes in terms of how their world shows up.

Imagine this woman's reaction when I said to her, "Try saying, 'There is never any shit in my life, only default-based projections based on my victim mentality.'"

When I use the expression "victim mentality," I mean feeling powerless to change a situation. As I went on to explain to this woman, "You are the creator of what has been happening to you."

I find so many of us don't want to own that *we're* the one who's creating our reality. We prefer to feel powerless to change our situation. The consequence is that we continue to hurt until we are finally willing to take back our power.

Rather than take responsibility for the choices we've made, we love to blame. Most of us are unable to face up to where we lack integrity and aren't committed because, to be so, we would need to take ownership of our behavior. Until we take responsibility for what's happening to us, we won't experience transformation.

I next asked this woman, "Did you choose to get married three times, yes or no? Did you know at the start, at some fundamental level, that something wasn't quite right, but you operated over the top of what you knew intuitively? Did you choose to have a child with this man? Did you choose to stay in a relationship where there were no boundaries on what's acceptable and unacceptable behavior? Did you choose to stay a victim, feeling powerless to change the situation? We are born free to choose and there are consequences for every choice we make. Now, tell me again, based on this new awareness, did you choose your life the way you've lived it?"

This isn't a message people who think of themselves as having been victimized or abused want to hear. Nevertheless, this woman signed on because she could see she had in fact created her reality and she was at last present to what it was costing her to live from her default identity.

Most of us who believe that "life is doing it to me" don't realize we are the one creating our misery. Then we have the gall to blame our parents, blame our siblings, blame our circumstances, and even blame Spirit for what *we* have chosen. In so doing, we abdicate responsibility for the choices we make. I did this for twenty years. The degree to which we abdicate responsibility is evidence of the degree to which we are locked into our default identity and therefore unconscious of our true being.

If we wish to change our circumstances, life requires us to change how we think and feel about ourselves. We have to allow our real self to determine our thoughts and emotions, not our default identity. The way we see the world and the way we feel about our life is exactly commensurate with the reality we experience. Sadly, most of us invest ourselves in thoughts and emotions that have no relevance other than the relevance we give them.

Why are so many of us wedded to *wanting* instead of to *committing?* Well, if we convince ourselves that happiness depends on our external circumstances changing, we aren't required to take responsibility. In other words, we like to abdicate responsibility for our happiness so we can avoid having to show up for the magnificent person we really are. As long as we are coming from our unconscious default identity, we can fly under the radar. We don't have to embrace our potential. Using the analogy of a tennis court, many are playing on the court called "want," wanting results that come only from the court called "committed." We can't produce the results that come from commitment unless we start playing on the committed court.

In a nutshell, we prefer not to be a Ten because Tens get noticed. Tens show up in the world. Many of us would *rather* live under the radar. It's as if we have a default-induced inability to be with "having it all." Most of us just don't believe we deserve to have it all. We'll see why this is the case in a later chapter.

It saddens me that even when we become aware, many of us choose to stay with the familiar. But as our default identity yields to our true being, having it all becomes a real possibility. It's the end of hurting and the fulfillment of our heart's desires.

four guiding principles for leading an empowered life

When human beings are disempowered, they tend to see things as very serious, significant, and dramatic. To free ourselves from the serious, significant, and dramatic, we need to realize that *only* four factors result in feeling disempowered. I have yet to come across someone who can identify any other factor that can render us disempowered. The four factors are:

- Fear
- The inner critic
- Framing life in terms of issues, problems, or challenges
- Confusion.

To use the analogy of a radio, these four factors are like the annoying static frequency we hear when we aren't properly tuned to a station. Because we don't get to appreciate the beauty of the music we are trying to listen to, it can't move us. These four factors are disempowering in the way that static spoils our experience of the program.

Whenever we are disempowered, we are actually unconsciously seeding a past or future-based projection. We add meaning to what's happening within a millisecond of experiencing fear, our inner critic, feeling stuck in the "how," or labeling our experience as an "issue," "problem," or "challenge." The language we use is key. As long as we talk about issues, problems, and challenges, we remain unaware of what's running the show.

A hundred percent of the time, it's a past or future-based projection that's at the root of our state, since there are *no* issues, problems, or challenges in real life, only projections. The inner critic doesn't exist except in the context of the meaning we add to what the voice says. When fear is present, we are either feeding something in the future that hasn't occurred, or we are dragging along something from the past. If we are stuck in the "how," all the obstacles we conjure up are nothing more than our projections, which of course allows us to abdicate responsibility.

What would your life look like if you no longer experienced anything as dramatic, serious, or significant? To live in an empowered state is to collapse the projections that create these interpretations of the events that occur in our lives.

The conscious mind goes through four *stages* in an instant and unconsciously. When we become aware of these stages, we can take our power back. The stages are:

- Recognition
- Evaluation
- Sensation
- Reaction.

When we are committed to learning to reframe the first two stages of conscious cognition, we create a different sensation, which leads to a conscious response instead of an unconscious reaction.

Chapter 5

a world where
nobody hurts
anymore

What would your life be like if you didn't hurt anymore?

For much of my life, I didn't know what it was *not* to hurt. Yet today, I no longer live in emotional pain. My world has been transformed beyond all recognition and I want to tell you how it happened.

I came to see that the countless ways in which we feel hurt by life ultimately come down to a single cause. Quite simply, we hurt because we are caught up in a negative emotional reaction.

To be human is to be triggered emotionally. Most of us are triggered by the various circumstances of our life on a moment-by-moment basis. We *live* in the trigger. And whenever we are triggered, we hurt.

Humans are walking triggers. For instance, we react to situations, either shooting off our mouth before we have a chance to think, kicking into defense mode, or becoming angry because of something someone said or did. The stock market plunges and we are in a panic. Our business slumps and we feel like a failure. Our car payment is due, things are tight, our partner was just laid off, so we feel life is treating us unfairly. Our spouse forgot to give us a kiss goodbye when they left for work this morning, we caught every red light on our drive, a critical email from our boss greeted us as we switched on our computer, so we feel mad at the world. In a thousand different ways, life triggers us.

We may fantasize that "someday" we might live beyond being triggered, but I've come to accept that life will always send us external circumstances that trigger us. Such situations are unavoidable for any human being.

If you're hoping to someday miraculously become a person who can no longer be triggered, it's likely you'll wait forever. To fantasize that you'll rise above being triggered if you pray enough for Spirit to keep you from being triggered, or meditate enough so you at last become a totally peaceful person who never reacts, you're simply fooling yourself.

The hope to reach a point we can't be triggered anymore is simply an unrealistic dream. No matter how many self-development programs I took, within a short time after returning home, I was being triggered just the way I'd always been triggered. The result was that I was soon hurting again.

In contrast, what *is* realistic is the possibility of self-mastery over being triggered.

When we are triggered, our response to the trigger doesn't have to become a life sentence. In other words, the key to self-mastery isn't that we can altogether avoid being triggered, it's the length of time we spend in our reactive mode. The mastery lies in the speed with which we move out of being triggered and back into our essential state of being.

a life of self-mastery

If you thought it was possible to feel a trigger and not have it take you over, what would this look like in practice?

You might feel anger arise in response to a trigger, but you would no longer be locked into venting that anger. You might at times feel alone, but you would never feel lonely. You might momentarily wonder whether you have the strength to handle a situation life has thrown at you, but you wouldn't function from a disempowered state. You would no longer tolerate being in dysfunctional relationships, no longer be thrown off kilter by the judgment of another human being, no longer operate from insecurity, no longer struggle interminably with overwhelming anxiety. Depression, addiction, or suicidal tendencies would never again wrap their tentacles around you and lock you in their grip.

There's a difference between either managing a trigger situation, or coordinating yourself around it, and completely detriggering. Complete detriggering is mastery. In the next chapter I'll show you how to achieve complete detriggering.

Learning to detrigger takes a little practice. Think back to when you first learned to drive. Initially the whole experience was rather confusing and your moves were somewhat clunky. Eventually driving became second nature, born from the self-interest of wanting to go places. In a similar way, learning to detrigger means moving from a state of unconscious incompetence to one of unconscious competence.

When we enter the realm of mastery, we're able to detrigger in an instant because our self-interest is in living a life in which we're free, a life in which absolutely nothing *has* us.

And I do mean nothing!

triggers are our access points

To engage in self-mastery is fundamentally different from the path many of us choose as we seek to escape pain. Instead we shut off our desires, shut down to our feelings, and close our heart so we don't risk feeling too deeply.

In this state, we are no longer full human beings. We have closed ourselves off to the essence of what humanness is, which is to feel the full experience of what it is to be alive.

Jill Bolte Taylor, a neuroanatomist affiliated with the Indiana University School of Medicine in Indianapolis and national spokesperson for the mentally ill at the Harvard Brain Tissue Resource Center, was named one of *Time* magazine's one-hundred most influential people in the world for 2008. In her book *My Stroke of Insight*, she explains: "Many of us think of ourselves as thinking creatures that feel, but biologically we are actually feeling creatures that think."

To feel is to be human.

Almost every course I took taught that thought precedes feeling. Science reveals just the opposite: being a feeling creature is what precipitates thought. Thought then compounds our emotional reaction.

Triggers actually serve a profound purpose in our life. They are the access point to empowered living in which we are present to the entirety of our life experience with the whole of our being.

Whenever we are triggered and consequently enter into an emotionally reactive state, we move away from the centered state of being we were in before the trigger took effect. But this state of being hasn't gone away—we have simply shifted out of it for a time. Although many on our planet spend much of their life in an emotionally reactive frame of mind, in none of us does the grounded state of being that precedes and underlies all of our reactions get destroyed. Hence, after a reaction has passed, we quite spontaneously return to this grounded state.

In other words, there's something more basic to our humanity than our triggered state—something enduring that's present in all of us. This deeper aspect of us simply becomes layered over with the reactivity that's responsible for all of our pain.

A person doesn't have to look far to realize that the fundamental nature of humanity is unconditional love. In our deepest being, at our most natural, we want to engage life and engage each other, sharing who we are with each other.

Name me a human being who, at their core, when their façade is down, doesn't want to experience unconditional love. The most hardened criminal in every prison on the planet longs to be loved unconditionally because they were never acknowledged, never validated, and never truly wanted. There isn't a human being alive who doesn't yearn to be accepted unquestioningly for who they *really* are.

At our center is an infinite ocean of love. It's the Source of our being, the very reason for the existence of the cosmos, and the essence of who each of us is individually.

Though we come into the world as expressions of love, we're like a baby with the potential to win an Olympic gold medal, but who can't even turn itself over at first, let alone stand up, walk, and run. Just as our physical potential is inherent and yet has to be developed in real-life experience, so too our basic nature of unconditional love has to be accessed, practiced, and finally established as our everyday reality.

Being triggered is how we learn to turn ourselves over, crawl, stand, walk, and run on the playground of love. By providing us with countless opportunities to become aware of the emotions we are experiencing, our triggers enable us to shift from emotional reactivity to real feelings of the heart. They give us the practice we need to sustain an openness to feel fully every aspect of our human journey.

Self-mastery is about how quickly we become aware we've been triggered and the length of time we spend in this triggered state—a few seconds, a minute, an hour, a day, a month, or longer. Some people go to their graves being triggered! Never expect not to experience triggers. We will experience triggers daily throughout our life—though when we reach the level of unconscious competency, it becomes increasingly possible to experience a trigger and not go into a reaction.

When we no longer react to situations negatively, we move from a deficit state, rooted in our default identity, into an asset-based state, grounded in our power. No longer dealing primarily with the drawbacks of our default identity, we're ready to embrace our strengths. We're ready to show up in life for the magnificent individuals we really are.

Imagine not only your own life free of pain, but an entire world that doesn't hurt anymore. The premise of such a world is that it's possible for the whole of the human experience to be based in love and only love.

In a world where people master their triggers and allow their inherent love to flow, there would be no need to manifest painful experiences such as war, poverty, pollution, or crime. We would live at a high level of consciousness, immersed in unconditional love.

Have you ever realized that we can't suffer unless we make things *mean* something? Can you imagine a world in which we no longer need to manifest adversity in order to learn? Having lived a life of extreme adversity, I now believe it was purely for the purpose of teaching people there's another way.

Chapter 6

it's all in what we make things *mean*

Have you ever really paused to recognize that our personal worlds are spun entirely from the meaning we give to the things that happen to us?

Even when we're certain we are seeing with perfect clarity, the world isn't the way we imagine it is. We are forever adding meaning to events, to the point that our default identity is nothing more than a learned mindset constructed from the meaning we've given to everything that's happened to us.

Living from a mindset in which we draw our meaning from our default identity, we operate predominantly from the way we've known ourselves and our world thus far. The meaning we add to events has nothing to do with the reality of the *now*. Rather it revolves around parts of ourselves that are unhealed from our childhood. More often than not, these are aspects of ourselves of which we have little if any awareness. Disconnected from our essence, which is always in the now, we live in either past or future-based projections and are hardly ever open to the potential of our present situation. We can't even *imagine* a different way of living our life.

why our past is important

I believe that if we are to enjoy the fulfillment of our inner being, which is the only way for us to invest ourselves in anything in a sustained way, it's essential we heal our childhood wounds. If we don't heal ourselves, our past will always be in our present, at least marring if not completely subverting the fulfillment we could be experiencing.

When we operate over the top of what's incomplete in us as most people do, we can't help but continually sabotage ourselves.

We've seen that to access our *being*, we need to *feel* again. This requires us to remove all blockages to feeling, which involves achieving completion with our parents or whoever were our primary male or female role models while we were growing up. If we are incomplete with either parent or whoever fulfilled this role for us, we'll also tend to experience difficulties with this gender in our adult life, which will hinder our ability to engage fruitfully in personal, social, and business relationships.

When I talk about healing our past, it's important to be aware that much of what goes under the banner of counseling to heal our past actually keeps our default state alive because its focus is on improving our existing paradigm instead of allowing this paradigm to disappear.

I have no interest in regurgitating the past. I'm simply interested in getting clear about what happened so we understand the dynamics involved then let them go. This allows us to take our power back, thereby making a difference that's sustainable. In other words, we go into our childhood, but only for the purpose of taking a snapshot of what happened and getting right back out so we can reclaim our power in the present.

When we put down solid foundations within our power-based identity, our default identity is no longer required. It dies a natural death, having accomplished what it was intended to accomplish, which was to keep us safe at a young age when we learned to believe life isn't safe. All default behavior begins as an attempt to protect ourselves in some way. Once we realize this, we are able to trust again. Because we trust, life becomes safe.

I was talking about how we attach meaning to events. Not only do we add our own meaning to events, others also seek to include us in their meaning. Whenever someone tries to draw us into their world of meaning, this is a moment to check we are in our power so we don't get sucked into doing battle with the other person's interpretation of reality.

Because people aren't used to engaging from their power, one person's disempowered state easily triggers another person to be disempowered. Part of what I train people to do is never to engage in dialogue with someone from their default, only from their power. This defuses any drama because the angst that produces drama can only occur when someone is making things mean something.

how to have a breakthrough

Let me illustrate how this works. In my seminars, the facilitators who work with me use flip charts to record the topics participants want me to address. In one such seminar, a woman asked that I talk about unplanned pregnancy. I inquired, "Are you pregnant and was it unplanned?"

"No," she responded, "I'm not pregnant, but I was unplanned." This woman was very evidently emotionally triggered by her unplanned birth. For forty-eight years she had been carrying this burden.

I asked her, "Would you like to have a breakthrough with this situation?" When she replied in the affirmative, I led her through a detriggering process that began with me asking her to describe what happened, which was of course that from her parents' point of view her birth was an accident.

Next I asked, "What have you made that mean?"

"I was a mistake," she said.

"And what did you make this mean about yourself?" I inquired.

It took only a few seconds for the woman to conclude, "I've always felt unlovable, like I'm not wanted."

When I inquired of this woman what she was getting out of feeding her belief that she wasn't wanted, her response was, "Nothing." Hers is a common response.

Whenever I have these conversations, the individual will say they are getting nothing out of their behavior. They are repeating behavior that never brings them what they seek, but they don't realize that they keep repeating this behavior because they are getting something from it.

Though a person may be unable to see what they are getting out of their behavior, they can always identify what it's costing them—what isn't happening in their life that they wish were happening, or what's happening that they would prefer not to be happening.

I asked this woman what her belief about herself as unlovable was costing her. She admitted that because she had cultivated an identity of being unlovable, she neither valued herself nor felt valued by others. "I'm sad," she said, looking forlorn, "and lonely." As she began to share what her life was like, it emerged she was also stressed, frustrated, and angry. Since so much of her energy was tied up in these negative emotions, she lacked vitality, felt tired much of the time, and was frequently depressed and at moments even suicidal. In reality, not a single aspect of her life was working.

What a price to pay, all because of a belief! Yet at some level we all pay a high price for our lack of awareness.

We don't transition successfully in the change process unless we are present to what we are getting out of our current beliefs and the behavior they generate. As long as we remain unaware of the benefits we're receiving, we are unable to make the change we seek and instead continue to hope it will somehow magically "appear" someday.

Encouraging this woman to develop awareness of her real state, I pressed, "How long have you been triggered by this situation?"

"All my life," she admitted.

"You might be getting something out of it then," I suggested.

Requesting she give only simple "yes" or "no" responses, I continued, "Do you get to be right and make your parents wrong? Do you get to be justified about your point of view? Do you get to be a victim, feeling powerless to change the situation? Do you get to avoid being responsible? Do you get to dominate, manipulate, and control?"

Her response to every single statement was affirmative. A look of realization dawned on her face. She was beginning to see how dissociated she had been from her true feelings.

I said to this woman, "Now you are aware of why your life hasn't been working, you have a choice. For instance, you are either committed to continuing to make your parents wrong or you are committed to transforming your life so you can experience love for the first time."

If we find ourselves stuck in our default mentality, unable to embrace a deeper awareness, it's always and only a function of the benefits we believe we derive from our present situation. If we were truly present to what our default behavior is costing us, we would move in a heartbeat.

This woman was married, had 2 children yet never experienced love and had no real relationship with her parents. All born out of a belief she was unlovable.

weighing the cost of our behavior

We are born with the capacity to choose, and our experiences are a direct reflection of the moment-by-moment choices we make.

Life's journey entails learning to make beneficial choices instead of choices programmed by past hurt. We accomplish this to the degree we become present to what our situation is costing us. Once we are aware, we have the ability to respond differently to *whatever* is occurring in our life.

Becoming present to the reality of our situation is the difficult step. Even when life takes a sledgehammer to us, some of us still have difficulty conceiving of ourselves in any way other than our default identity. I think of a woman in her late forties whose husband literally went after her with a sledgehammer, fracturing her skull and putting her in the hospital for the next three months. No sooner was she released than she was back with him.

"Why?" I asked when she came to talk with me during the break at one of my keynotes.

"Because I'm terrified of him," she said.

It might seem being terrified is the very reason not to return to a wife beater. But when being terrified has become a woman's default identity, it's all she knows and therefore seems "normal" to her.

When we put a label on our state of mind, we somehow feel safer because at least we now have an identity of sorts. As a defense against her fear, this woman had created for herself the identity of a "fearful" person. Her fear stemmed from being sexually molested as a child, a fear that had never been healed. To maintain this default identity, she had to place herself in a situation that kept her in a terrified state all the time. This is why she was willing to return to a marital home in which there were no boundaries for what was acceptable and unacceptable behavior. Her marriage replicated the upbringing that had provided her with no boundaries when she was a child. It was the only reality she knew, the only way she could feel any sort of comforting familiarity.

When I asked her what meaning she had given to her husband's bludgeoning of her, her response was, "All I ever do is try my best to please him. What have I done to deserve something this awful?" In other words, she felt the violence was her fault. She believed she deserved it in some way. The reason she believed she could never please anyone was that this was her experience in the home in which she grew up, which caused her to choose a husband she in fact could never please.

As we talked, this woman became present to the fact she made the choice to live with this man, then eventually marry him, all the while knowing he was violent. She also became present to the fact that, despite everyone in her wider family trying to persuade her not to go back to him after leaving the hospital, she chose to go back. She was behaving like a victim who was powerless to change her situation.

It may surprise you to learn that I'm talking about an educated person who works in the mental health sector and who was dealing with issues of this nature in the lives of others. This was a case of the wounded supporting the wounded, a phenomenon I observe quite often. How many abused women on the planet keep going back like this?

Until a person realizes their behavior stems from a need to feed their fear—to recreate a familiar feeling from childhood—they continue to compound their terror by placing themselves at risk. As author Caroline Myss says, until we claim our power we don't meet our soul mate, we meet our wound mate. One of the reasons I'm able to help people in such situations is that I was a "woundologist" for twenty years without realizing it. You meet and connect at a wound level, not a soul level.

the pitfall of seriousness

A clear signal we are giving meaning to something is that we notice ourselves being serious, significant, and dramatic. These are functions of our default identity.

Such states *always* involve a past or future-based projection. In fact, I believe there are no issues, problems, or challenges in life, *only* projections.

When fear is present, we are either feeding a projection into the future, which clearly hasn't occurred, or we are dragging something in from the past, which we believe we can't change. In other words, the things we frame as issues, problems, and challenges are all symptoms of the fact we aren't *present*.

I was the queen of seriousness, significance, and drama. I lived my life in extreme fear, experiencing anxiety attacks on a daily basis. There were what I saw as issues, problems, and challenges in every area of my life, and I was always confused as to why my life wasn't working. I didn't realize this was happening because, from my default identity's perspective, it was exactly what I needed in order to fly under the radar and not have to show up. I had a need to validate my default way of understanding myself, so I was always gathering evidence for this mindset.

How many people do you know in your life who are fearful, who always have issues, problems, and challenges, who live in confusion, and for whom so much of life is serious, significant, and dramatic?

What would your own life look like if you no longer experienced being serious, significant, and dramatic?

no such thing as a hopeless case

If we once see that when anything happens in our life, we create worlds with no substance other than the validity we ascribe to them, we have the option to die to all such meaning. We stop feeding past or future projections by adding meaning to things that happen to us and begin living in the *now,* free of default-based interpretations.

Some have lived so many years in a frozen state that we write them off as unreachable in this life. "Oh, he's so closed off he'd never 'get it' in a million years," we tell ourselves. In actuality, it's often the individuals who appear to be the most shut down who make the best candidates for awakening to their true self.

I believe a person can have a breakthrough on any perceived issue no matter how long they have felt stuck.

How transformation can follow rapidly once we're present to our default mindset and what it's costing us can be seen in the case of a board member in a company run by seven executive board members. This woman was on her way out because the board disliked her, the staff disliked her, customers disliked her, and the CEO was at his wits' end after employing every skill he possessed to try to rectify the situation. But even though the executive was utterly dysfunctional in an executive role, the CEO wanted to try one last approach: coaching.

It was important to involve the whole board in the coaching, not just the executive who was having so much difficulty. I was delighted that the CEO and other board members agreed to participate. Whenever I take on any client, it has to be through free choice. An organization can't say to someone, "You are going to be coached." Consequently, I met individually with all six executives, each of whom chose to enter the program individually.

The CEO kept reaffirming what a challenge it was going to be to deal with this executive. Yet I found the executive was the easiest to deal with. Why? Because she was in the most pain! She had reached the lowest point possible, which meant anything other than what she was experiencing was great.

The irony is that the only thing this woman was interested in was love, though she wasn't experiencing it in any area of her life. She had a poor relationship not just with her peers, her staff, and her customers, but also with her husband and children. In fact, no area of her life was working. She had even abdicated all knowledge of her financial situation by having her husband manage the finances so she could make him "wrong" when things didn't pan out as they planned.

It didn't take long for the executive to recognize the cost of what was showing up in her life. She readily admitted she was dying inside, though she had no idea how to change things. With this admission, we went to work on having her face up to the kind of person she was being in all areas of her life. She did this bravely, apologizing for who she had been and completing any conversations that needed to be completed. The change in her demeanor as a result was huge. She became a functional wife and mother, a valuable contributor to the executive team, an inspiration to the staff, to the point that some of her staff came to my seminars and said to me, "I enrolled in this course because if you were able to help this woman transform her life, it's possible for anyone to change. None of us believed it was doable when you first set out."

I put to you that those we perceive as the most dysfunctional in our personal or corporate environment are actually the most malleable, but we have them locked in a default identity largely of our own making.

After this woman's transformation, the CEO talked with me about the process that brought about such a change. I said to him, "This woman will have no difficulty sustaining her change and moving forward because she has known the worst. She is so present to the cost."

It's easy to write off the most cynical, skeptical, shut down, angry, or negative people, yet I have found these are some of the most likely to change once they gain the required insight.

Chapter 7

embrace your
saboteur

To be human is to have an inner critic. Unless we've undertaken a measure of self-development through which we've become acquainted with this inner critic, most of us tend to be quite unaware of the destructive role it plays in our life.

Our inner critic is a saboteur. Allowed free rein, it annihilates human potential.

Self-improvement programs that draw awareness to our inner critic generally teach tools for managing it. We learn how to coordinate ourselves around its destructive voice. This is ultimately of limited effect because the control we achieve is still part of our default identity.

What I'm interested in is how to "disappear" the inner critic.

We each experience our inner critic at a different volume. I've noticed that the degree to which we step out in life, going for the things we want, affects the level at which our inner critic rages at us.

I think of clients who for forty, fifty, or sixty years have denied themselves the life they really wanted because they listened to this critical internal voice. For instance, a lawyer watched a New Zealand television *60 Minutes* documentary about the traumatic experience I went through, an experience I'll share with you in due course. He was so affected by the documentary, he made an appointment with me to talk about his inability to deal with his inner critic. He had never come across anybody who addresses it in the way I do, so for the first time he felt someone might actually understand him. "Teach me how to silence my inner critic," he said, "because it has denied me my life."

This man was sixty years old, so you would think he would do anything for a breakthrough. He certainly said he would. Yet he never signed on. Surprised? When I highlighted for him the part he was playing in the dynamic of his inner critic, he didn't want to take hold of this insight. Victims resist taking their power back because once they do, life will ask them to show up, and showing up scares us because it requires us to journey into unfamiliar territory.

To get across to clients the consequences of being aware but not shifting into actual consciousness, I ask them whether they are child abusers. You can imagine their response! A hundred percent of the time, it's an emphatic, "No!"

So then I ask, "If a child were sitting beside you right now, would you berate that child the way you berate yourself most days?"

They respond, "Oh God, no!"

Next I ask, "So why do you do this to yourself? What have you done that was so bad as to warrant decades of abuse?"

the most important tool of all

Surveying self-development programs, it seems to me there's a lack of emphasis on the one area that will hinder anyone from accomplishing what they want more than anything else. Every course I ever went on, I was given tools that were meant to help me change my life. Many of them were actually helpful tools. But I wasn't given the tools to deal with the fear that caused my inner critic to stop me in my tracks again and again.

Even though fear is fundamental to the human predicament, not one teacher said to me, "If you master your fear, you will silence your inner critic. Fear is the only thing that can stop you achieving what you want. Embrace fear and the world is your oyster."

To recognize that our inner critic is fueled by fear is the most important tool of all if we are ever to become what we came to Earth to be.

I had the most vicious inner critic for more than thirty years. It never let up on me 24/7. I functioned under a tirade of the worst possible self-generated language that, omitting the expletives, ran along the following vein: "Who do you think you are? What do you imagine you can *ever* do in your life that can be of any value? What man would want a woman like you? You're scum, dirt, sub-human." As a consequence, I often thought I was going mad—and in some ways, it *was* like having multiple personalities, as I will share with you in the latter part of this book.

Ask yourself this question: What have you ever done in your life to deserve years, if not decades, of internal abuse? And what could you achieve if you no longer listened to your destructive inner critic?

I can tell you that "disappearing" my own inner critic has totally transformed my life.

the resist-persist syndrome

There are four steps to disappearing our inner critic, the first of which is awareness. Having said this, let me caution you that if you imagine just being aware will enable you to take back your power, you'll find it's not that simple. This is because, once we become aware, we experience a resist-persist syndrome.

Why does awareness trigger resistance?

When we first discover the extent to which we have unwittingly surrendered control of our life to our critic, it's quite shocking. We tend to feel so confronted that we don't know how to move forward. We realize we have limited ourselves in so many ways, and we feel paralyzed in the face of what seems like overwhelming odds that we could ever really make something of our life.

When we begin asserting our true self, the critic increases its volume in a mistaken attempt to keep us from failing. It scolds: "Who do you think you are, some kind of big shot?" It's a protective mechanism. We tell ourselves it's hopeless to imagine we're ever going to achieve our desires, then lapse into a victim mentality that will forever challenge us. There's a certain comfort in being a victim!

I used to associate being a victim with being weak. Then I realized that victimhood is feeling powerless to change a particular *situation,* but not at all a *state* of powerlessness. On the contrary, our sense of victimhood has a powerful grip on us it doesn't want to release.

Once I recognized this, I realized that *I,* in my innate power, was in fact at the core of my dysfunctional behavior. This is because we can never not be powerful. We are powerful, and our power is going to be invested somewhere. It's only a question of how it's going to be deployed.

Let me say this again because it's so crucial: To be a victim is a powerful role—albeit a highly protective, defensive role. All the antics of our default identity are actually powerful ways of protecting ourselves.

I came to see I was playing a powerful part by criticizing myself and thereby keeping *myself* stuck. I wondered why I wasn't in a relationship, why I didn't have enough money, why I couldn't stop smoking. But all the time it was *I* who was keeping these states in place. What we most complain about is what we are most committed to!

The biggest thing with any victim behavior is that we don't want to give up *seeming* powerless in a situation. In fact, we love appearing powerless. "Look what they are doing to me!" we exclaim as we amass enough justification for pitying ourselves to sink a ship. Then we complain, "I can't change the situation!" But when we experience an internal shift, our perception of our "problem" shifts too.

Which is why if a mother brings her raped daughter to see me, I explain to the mother off the back of my own experience, "I am only interested in breakthrough results. For such results to be experienced, the individual needs to own the part they play in what they attract. This is the most difficult aspect for people to understand." We can only have a breakthrough with our victim status if we're willing to own up to the part we're playing in what's happening in our life. Victims don't want to hear this.

Feeling sorry for someone in pain, empathizing with what happened and how it happened, does nothing to move a person beyond their pain. This is a hard statement for people to wrap their head around, especially when they want to dwell on how atrocious the experience was. I call this *rescuing* someone, and this doesn't serve the person.

Part of the attraction of supporting someone in their victim's story is that the listener is able to avoid looking at *themselves*. They hear a horrific story and feel sorry for the person, which deflects their entire focus onto the victim. I admit that this is a generalization, and yet it's evident in what I witness as a coach and have seen to be the case in my own life experience.

On occasion, I have received feedback that a participant in one of my workshops felt sorry for me. Being treated as if you are your wound i n s u l t s who you truly are in your essence.

A victim identity doesn't want to be edged out. So the more we battle our inner critic, the stronger it becomes. The stronger it becomes, the more we resist it. And what we resist persists. So the way forward is *sustained* awareness that's also focused on our resistance.

Because it's an issue that often causes confusion, let me say what I've just said in a slightly different way: The key to ending the tyranny of our inner critic isn't to fight it but to become a silent observer. Indeed, it's crucial to make *no* attempt to change the voice in our head. Rather, if we observe what we tell ourselves in a sustained way, and also quietly observe our resist-persist tendency, the voice in our head gradually loses its power over us. We see our inner critic for what it really is: an empty threat to our magnificent potential.

evidence to the contrary

As we observe the voice in our head, a second phase of this process kicks in quite spontaneously. We don't have to do anything, it just begins happening. Evidence start showing up that contradicts what our inner critic says.

As this evidence begins trickling into our life, it causes us to reshape how we understand ourselves. The amount of contrasting evidence we receive will be in direct proportion to the degree to which we realign our efforts with what we say we are committed to. Eventually, as the flow of evidence becomes a torrent, it proves to be more than the inner critic can counter, which causes our saboteur to lose its power.

Actually, our situation becomes humorous, as I experienced in my own case. Having failed academically at school, I labeled myself "dumb" for the next two decades. Only when I was asked to speak to some sixty MBA students about my international corporate career did I realize the ridiculousness of typecasting myself as dumb when these brilliant students were hanging on my every word.

How different this is from trying to "manage" the inner critic or work around it. When we bring awareness to this destructive voice, engaging in nothing other than sustained observing, it deteriorates into a mere death rattle and ultimately disappears altogether.

dark side integration

I call phase three of this process Dark Side Integration. During this phase, we learn to embrace the focus point of our inner critic. We face our fears and see them for what they really are, which is nothing but a projection. As such, they exist only in our head. Consequently, what we dwell on is what we create in our everyday lives. This is how powerful we are.

To help us get a sense of balance, we tend to want to see the world in terms of opposites. We like to think of reality as up-down, big-small, back-forward, in-out, sweet-bitter, hard-soft, and light-dark. In actuality, the world isn't this way. It isn't black and white. In fact, few things exist at the extremes, with most falling somewhere in between. Look around you and you'll see that black and white form only a small portion of what our eyes take in. Touch the things around you, and you'll realize there's a vast spectrum of hardness and softness.

When people imagine they live in a world of opposites, they don't realize they are polarized. For instance, to a person who belongs to the political right, this is the only world that exists for them. They can't imagine embracing any of the tenets of the left since these seem anathema to everything they believe makes for a good life. Similarly, those on the left can't entertain the worldview of the right. What's lacking at both extremes is the ability to realize that any polarized mindset is far from whole.

In the realm of the unconscious mind, certain human traits are labeled sub-personalities. There are light side sub-personalities and dark side sub-personalities. On the light side are such characteristics as passion, excitement, vitality, power, laughter, compassion, and joy. On the dark side are judgment, assessment, criticism, anger, domination, control, and aggression. When we see ourselves in terms of polarities, we embrace some aspects of ourselves and reject other aspects as our "dark side." We have a hard time being with both kinds of traits.

To reintegrate back into being whole and complete, we must fall in love with what we perceive as dark. We must embrace those aspects of ourselves in which we feel somehow less than we imagine we ought to be.

While for years I lived in paradigms of right versus wrong, good versus bad, should versus shouldn't, today I choose not to live in the realm of polarized extremes. I don't want to hate or shun any part of myself. I choose not to live in any measure of self-rejection because to function as a Ten requires me to embrace the whole of myself.

When we decide to embrace every aspect of ourselves, including our so-called dark side, we learn compassion for ourselves. Becoming compassionate toward ourselves in turn leads to a new self-love, which as we saw earlier is actually nothing more than becoming aware of the love we innately have for ourselves—the love that is our essence, which we can in fact never escape. Since love is the ultimate value in the universe from which everything has been birthed, this revival of self-love is accompanied by an increase in our perception of our self-worth.

How can we accept those parts of ourselves in which we feel inadequate?

Consider how an orchestra has many members, each playing different instruments at different levels of experience. Not everyone gets to play first fiddle. For an orchestra to play beautiful music, all its members must find their appropriate part and play this part with all their being. When each member of an orchestra accepts their role, their weaknesses are transmuted into an alchemical harmony.

Similarly, there are many players on a sports team, each with different positions, different degrees of expertise, and different gradations of experience. Not everyone can be a good center forward, goal keeper, batsman, or pitcher. For the team to win the game, they must each fully embrace their particular skill, not berating themselves because they aren't good in another position on the field, thereby transcending any perceived lack as they function as a unified team.

We are each the conductor of our orchestra, the coach of our sports team. To hear the music or win the game, we need to fall in love with that which we perceive as dark as much as with that which we perceive as light. When we do so, what we perceive as dark within ourselves becomes the access point to the light.

The golden rule is that anything we are unable to *be with* will *have* us.

The gold lies in the ability to be with both what is *and* what isn't, without imparting some kind of meaning to the fact that something is or isn't. We accept that, for now, it just *is*. When we do, so an alchemical change gets underway that transmutes everything into an expression of love. Once we shine the light on anything that's dark, it can no longer exist: it's always transmuted into love.

The journey into consciousness involves first becoming a spotlight, shining the light on that which is dark in our lives, then becoming a beacon to share our light with the world.

the power of liberating oneself

Sometimes our critic turns on someone else and we experience an impulse to judge them. If we are aware, in the moment we're tempted to judge/point a finger, we'll recognize there are three fingers pointing back at ourselves.

Here is where the alchemy happens. We find ourselves asking of our judging: what does this say about *me?*

In the moment we are angry, asking ourselves what our anger says about *us* becomes our access point to shift our state. The realization dawns, "I'm not committed to being angry. What then am I committed to? I'm committed to asserting my loving self." In other words, anger is transmuted into showing up in our life for the loving person we really are. We move through the dark to the light.

One of the most moving group facilitation conversations I have ever experienced was with a man who was forty-five years old and had one child. Just looking at him in the audience, I could sense some dark secret in him. Hoping he would step forward, I asked, "Who wants a breakthrough in their life in an area where they have never had a breakthrough? I don't care how dark your issue appears. I don't care whether you have fed it for decades. If you want to have a breakthrough in just thirty minutes, come to the front of the room."

Most of us are terrified to expose those areas of our life where we have never experienced a breakthrough. This man was nervous to the point of shaking, which gave me some idea of how dark his perceived issue was. When he volunteered, I explained to him there was nothing he could share that would faze me—nothing. You'll appreciate what I mean when you hear his story.

I began by inquiring, "Do I have permission to ask any question required for you to have a breakthrough?" He gave his permission. I teach facilitators that we have no right to explore someone's personal history unless we have their approval. The person has to be ready to look. He was ready because he was in a lot of pain.

I requested that he describe the three worst incidents he had experienced in childhood. Instantly, tears filled his eyes. You could have heard a pin drop in the room. This strong, stalwart man was actually incredibly vulnerable!

His first recollection was of being molested by his uncle at age five, in response to which he described himself as "angry." His second recollection was of being left alone in the house as a young child because his parents were alcoholics and always at the local bar. Terrified of being alone, he described himself as "scared and lonely." His third recollection was of witnessing his father beating his mother to the point she was brain-damaged, which caused him to hit his father over the head with a beer bottle, a blow that almost ended his father's life. As a result, from age twelve onward he had thought of himself as "bad."

At this point the man was openly crying. From age twelve to age forty-five, he had told not a soul about these incidents. For thirty-three years, he had believed he was a bad person, terrified that if anyone found out about his past, he would end up alone. All these years he had been living out of a belief that had no validity. Can you imagine how it felt for him to have a breakthrough after more than three decades locked up inside himself?

In front of the live audience, I facilitated the detriggering process. When I facilitate, I remain calm, neutral, unfazed, and intensely present. I listen for the person's greatness unlike anybody has listened for their greatness before. I'm not swayed by their emotion; on the contrary, I hand them a box of tissues and keep going. I've learned that as a facilitator, if I'm swayed by the individual's emotion, the group will be swayed. I'm keenly aware that as well as facilitating the individual in front of me, I'm also managing the group. Who I am is who they will be. Because I stay calm, the group remains calm.

I inquired of this man, "What is the 'what happened?'"

"I witnessed my father physically abusing my mother."

"What did you make that mean?"

He began describing his response to his father's actions: "Get off her you bastard! How dare you treat my mother like that? Who do you think you are? You can't do that to my mother!"

I asked the question more specifically: "What did you make that mean about *yourself?*"

This time the answer came back unequivocally: "I'm bad because I nearly killed my father."

I then asked him, "When was the last time you spoke to your father as a son would normally talk to his father?"

"Thirty-three years ago," he said, sobbing.

I continued, "Would you like to know what you are getting out of it? Do you get to be right and make your father wrong? Do you get to be justified about your point of view? Do you feel like a victim, powerless to change the situation? Do you get to dominate, manipulate, and control because you can't condone what happened? I'm talking about how you removed yourself from your father's life. I'm not condoning what happened. I'm saying you've controlled the outcome by feeding what happened for more than three decades. What's it costing you?"

The cost was clear to him now: "I don't have a relationship with my father. As a result, there's a lack of love, connection, and intimacy in all my relationships. I feel sad, lonely, even suicidal at times. I feel frustrated and angry." He told of how his predicament was affecting his vitality, his energy. So what he had made his past mean wasn't only costing him his relationship with his father, it was costing him any meaningful relationship with his wife and his son. He lived in terror he might become a bad husband and a bad father like his own father.

"Now that you are aware of what happened," I said, "are you willing to forgive and become responsible? Because the cost of feeding something for thirty-three years is too great. And it's not even mainly about forgiving your father. It's ten percent him and ninety percent yourself for what you've done to yourself all these years."

People are often reluctant to forgive because they think to do so is to condone what happened. We are unlikely to forgive when our focus is on the act that was committed. As long as our focus is on the act, we're going to feel as though we have to condone it to forgive. Since we can't get our head around how we can condone it, we stay stuck in unforgiveness. In no way do I condone the atrocities people perpetrate. However, it isn't the act we're forgiving, it's the person. To forgive by no means condones the person's behavior. Rather, it honors the *real* person behind the behavior that needs forgiveness. A conscious individual listens for the real person instead of focusing on the default behavior, keenly aware that the real person is magnificent, then manages the default behavior separately.

I challenged this man, "Are you now willing to choose a new way of being, based on your awareness? Are you committed to having a great relationship with your father so you can find the freedom to love in all your relationships?" At this point he broke down completely.

I also distinguished for this man that he had shown no compassion for the twelve-year-old boy who was trying to save his mother. He had made himself wrong for decades, yet in fact he had done nothing wrong.

This man has since reconciled with his father.

Imagine how many breakthroughs occurred in that room that day out of the vulnerability of this individual's sharing. People could put themselves in his shoes, thereby transmuting into light whatever dark dynamic they were running in their own life. What have you been feeding for decades that has no validity other than what you gave it as a child?

Think about the number of people who hold secrets and don't say what's happening to them. It's all kept in the dark because of the shame. When we shine the light on every dark crevice of the psyche, we realize the only power the dark holds over us is the power we give it by not embracing it and bringing it into the light.

What's the first thing people do when they are confronted, feel resistance, or are fearful? They hightail it out of the situation. In contrast, I train people to *go into* what they are avoiding in just the way I took this man into what he'd been avoiding. If you no longer want to experience anything of a dark nature, *go into it*. Don't avoid it, but instead embrace it. Go to that which you avoid and see it for what it really is: a distortion of love.

To be compassionate doesn't mean we allow ourselves to be harmed or have to live in the same house as a person who's creating hell for themselves. The key is to put a clear boundary in place on what's acceptable and unacceptable behavior. Even if we choose to move out, we do so as an act of compassion, not with anger, resentment, and bitterness.

A person who operates from their default identity isn't used to experiencing love when they are in a judgmental mode. Hence, the more we come from love in the face of projection, the more likely we are to elicit a beneficial result. For this reason, I listen to the person's greatness but have compassion for where they are presently operating. The more heinous the dialogue, the more I have a chance to identify the source of the person's pain.

judgment is an opportunity to master compassion

When we feel someone is judging us, we usually find ourselves triggered into default behavior. The reason we are triggered is that we take on the default projection from the other person.

Know that when someone specifically aims judgment at you personally, it *never* has anything to do with you. Once we really get this, we don't become triggered to the point of reacting. We remain in our true state instead of shifting into our default identity. By short-circuiting our tendency to react from our default, we create a window through which we can ascertain the real issue that's seeking to be communicated, which opens the way for us to be compassionate in a constructive manner.

When we don't allow ourselves to be triggered by the judgment being meted out, it confuses the person who is in their default identity because they are used to engaging at a default-to-default level. The individual finds themself out on a limb all alone because we won't go there with them. Since they are alone in their judgment, they get to see the contrast between their highly charged projections and our calm presence.

By responding in such a way, we don't return judgment for judgment. Anticipating they will receive judgment is half the reason people don't show up. Who is going to want to show up when they know they are going to be judged, assessed, or criticized? By not returning judgment, we give the judgmental person's true self a chance to show up.

This is how a breakthrough can happen, whereas if we react, we siphon off any possibility of such an awakening. It's powerful to alter someone else's state simply as a function of who we are *being,* instead of forever trying to change them.

We know when we have mastered compassion by the fact we are able to be with every single atrocity on the planet—pedophilia, incest, rape, murder, war, poverty—without judgment. We are simply compassionately present with those who are hurting so much that they do terrible things to others.

If judgment can teach us how to become masters of compassion, imagine what an atmosphere of love could do for us.

When we embrace the dark side, the uncomfortable becomes the new comfortable. Then it becomes humorous because we realize we've lived perhaps years or decades in a state of being "had" by a thought to which we gave validity, but that has no actual substance. What a joke! We did this to ourselves because the thoughts and emotions we feed—the things we believe in—are what show up as our everyday reality.

Fear is our barometer of how disconnected we are from our Source. When fear is present, love is in hiding. When love is in hiding, we perceive Spirit as hidden from us. The speed with which we reconnect with our loving Source speaks volumes about our commitment to our spiritual evolution.

connecting to others requires us to connect to ourselves

The fourth phase of embracing our inner critic involves transitioning from lower level consciousness to higher level consciousness. I'm talking about the difference between being aware, and awareness reaching the point of critical mass so we actually go through a metamorphosis.

Few of us are aware of how our language reflects where our real commitment lies. However, if you listen to people who label themselves "seekers," you'll notice how they language their world in the following kinds of ways: I don't have enough money, I don't have enough time, I don't have enough energy, I don't know what I'm passionate about. By using throwaway lines like these— statements the inner critic thrives on because we're actually judging ourselves to be inadequate—we get to abdicate responsibility.

But we can change all of this. We can stop abdicating responsibility and share our magnificence with the world by connecting with our true being and committing to showing up in every aspect of our life.

As an example of what a difference it makes when we connect with ourselves and commit to showing up, I had the privilege of coaching a friend's father who, when I met him, didn't value himself at all. He had left school at thirteen and pretty much branded himself as unworthy of either love or success. His entire life, he hadn't given to himself because he didn't feel worthy. He couldn't even articulate his dreams and desires because he believed it wasn't possible for him to make something of himself.

This man had raised four amazing children, yet he couldn't bring himself to hug his children. They were especially disappointed that he vowed he would never speak at any of their wedding receptions. He told himself he had nothing worth sharing. Yet he desperately wanted to enjoy a deeper connection with his family.

We went to work on identifying his beliefs and at the same time identifying what he wanted. He said he might like to run his own business in the concrete industry. As he became present to the cost of not valuing himself, I asked him to think about something opulent that would quantify his value. So deeply entrenched was his lack of self-worth that it was an arduous process to get him to even say what he wanted. Finally, he decided he would love to buy a pair of Italian shoes, have an Italian suit tailored, and speak at his youngest daughter's wedding.

Every time he turned up for coaching, the man came in his truck and gumboots. But what I observed wasn't his external appearance. I saw the level of wisdom he exuded from having raised four children. This is because I look for people's greatness, which is their true being, instead of focusing on their default identity. It was a privilege to be in this man's presence as he acknowledged what it was like for   a sixty-five-year-old man to come to the place he was willing to change.

Each time he left a session, when I went to hug him, he deflected the hug. I asked him, "Is that how you always hug? What's it like being around your children if you can't hug them, let alone your grandchildren?"

How someone hugs another human being is indicative of their level of connection to *themselves.*

Little by little, I taught this man how to hug someone and hold them long enough to connect. Slowly, he began to realize it was safe to connect. To see this man surrender to being contributed to in a simple hug was moving. It was in surrendering to being hugged that he learned he was of value.

One day the man showed up in Italian shoes and an Italian suit. What a contrast! He looked proud beyond words. We went to work on crafting a speech. Until the day of his daughter's wedding, my client's family had only known a quiet man who was extremely reserved. Now they witnessed him walk into the room with pride. No one knew what was coming. First he addressed the wedding party, sharing from his heart, apologizing to his other children for not speaking at their weddings and explaining why. His presence commanded the attention of the entire room and there wasn't a dry eye to be seen. This family were seeing their father reclaim his power.

This man went on to start his own consulting practice for a concrete company, charging several times more than he had earned before. The fundamental lesson is that until we silence our inner critic and at last value ourselves, we'll never get what we want.

The paradox in all this is that the inner critic doesn't actually exist. It has no real substance and is nothing but a construct of thought and emotion whose purpose is to keep us disconnected from our true being and keep us safe, but in a dysfunctional way.

By tuning into the inner critic's frequency, we remain disconnected from our Source. How convenient! We can go about our life telling ourselves we are on a spiritual journey, but we never actually become spiritual, never actually live consciously. A spiritual life remains wishful thinking, our plan for "someday."

there will come a day in my lifetime

There will come a day in my lifetime where mastery of the inner critic will be part of the core curriculum in the schooling system. To be human is to have an inner critic, yet almost nobody talks about it. Why is that? Can you imagine a world in which humans no longer experience such destructive internal dialogue? It breaks my heart when I talk to an eight-year-old girl about how powerful her inner critic is and she doesn't know how to deal with it.

Returning to the analogy of a radio station with static in the background, the static is like our inner critic. As long as we are hearing the static of this critic, we lack clarity about our life's purpose. However, when we are properly tuned into a station that's playing beautiful music, it calms, centers, and inspires us. The music is like our intuition, which offers us clear direction.

To take this analogy a step further, we can choose to tune into a frequency with a lot of static or we can choose to tune into a frequency that plays crystal clear music. Which we choose to listen to reveals where our commitment lies. When we are aware, yet willingly continue to choose a frequency that no longer serves us, it tells us we like confusion because it allows us to keep our default perspective in place.

Of the research I have conducted in the area of the inner critic, I have never found anything that speaks of complete liberation from this voice. Most teach how to manage the voice or co-ordinate ourselves around it, but none speak of silencing it. One technique quite amused me. Why on Earth would someone put a rubber band on their wrist and flick it every time they experience their inner critic? Apparently their inner critic hasn't yet inflicted enough pain!

Chapter 8

get acquainted
with your greatness

When I talk to people about their magnificence, they look at me like I'm psychotic. It's as if they are saying of themselves, "How can I be magnificent when I've been trying to fix myself for twenty years and still have so far to go?"

We were born magnificent, but then adopted what became our default identity. When we are in our default state of mind, we can't tolerate the knowledge we are magnificent. And when we're unable to acknowledge ourselves for the magnificent person we are, no amount of acknowledgment from others will alter how we feel.

I conduct a lot of workshops, so I come across a lot of people who have low self-esteem. Thinking of themselves as magnificent is a real challenge for many who attend these workshops. Quite apart from being unable to acknowledge their own greatness, they feel embarrassed and awkward when they receive a compliment from others. This isn't surprising, because only to the degree we can acknowledge ourselves without needing the validation of others will we be comfortable with the wonderful things people have to say about us.

When we receive acknowledgment, many of us tend to deflect the compliment we're being given. We can't be *with* it, so we cut the person off at the knees. Even when we train ourselves to say "thank you" rather than rebuffing a compliment, we probably feel uncomfortable. Still, we say "thank you" because we realize it's of benefit to us to express gratitude.

When we are at last able to own acknowledgement, it's the divine in us that acknowledges the divine in the one acknowledging us. We can own what the individual is seeing in us, and we can own it without reservation or qualification. In fact, acknowledgment helps us see where our strengths truly lie. We stop feeling sheepish and apologetic about being the gifted individual we are.

an exercise in acknowledging ourselves

The journey from hearing acknowledgment of our greatness and feeling uncomfortable, to finally owning how wonderful we are and appreciating it when others recognize this, is one of dying to our sense of inadequacy and embracing who we really are in our essence.

To help my clients embrace acknowledgment, I invite them to write down a hundred things they would like to be acknowledged for in their life up to this point. With few exceptions, people don't manage to get beyond about forty items. They experience a resistance to writing down this many ways in which they would like to be acknowledged. If a person is forty years old, for instance, and can't even write down a hundred ways they wish to be acknowledged, it's a direct indicator of a lack of self-worth.

The manner in which clients respond to this request is indicative of their degree of dissociation from their true being. This is evident from the two standard responses I hear.

The first way in which people tend to respond is by listing items that begin: "Jane would like to be acknowledged for..." Notice the person doesn't say "I." Men and women both tend to use their name, which is to ask for acknowledgment in a dissociated fashion. To say "I" is too direct, too personal for an individual who has low self-esteem.

The second response generally takes the form of a statement such as: "I'm a good friend. I'm a good cook. I'm a good gardener." This tells me nothing about the person as a being. In other words, the responses I receive are usually based in the individual's default identity—roles, not personal experiences. Yet the purpose of the exercise is to help people become present to their magnificence *quite apart from what they have learned to do well.* A person might do all kinds of things well and still feel inadequate or inferior.

When individuals move into a feeling state, what they write about themselves changes. Instead of writing, "I'm a good friend," they write something like: "I want to be acknowledged for being there for John four years ago when he was going through his divorce."

When I first ask people to acknowledge themselves, they view it as selfish and egoic. Somewhere in their life, they've learned we aren't supposed to view ourselves as wonderful and certainly not supposed to promote ourselves. In other words, people don't realize there's a world of difference between feeding the ego and celebrating our greatness. To feed the ego is to pump up something imaginary because the ego is nothing more than how we've learned to think about ourselves. To celebrate our greatness is to recognize what *is*.

It's our birthright to be great. We are magnificent. Consequently, there's nothing to "fix" about us. But if we've spent decades believing we're not good enough, we'll act out what we believe about ourselves— and then we make a mess of our life, which leads to feeling broken and spawns the belief we need serious fixing. So now we spend decades trying to fix ourselves through various self-help methodologies, when all we need is to remember who we are—who we were as a child before we bought into the false beliefs we hold about ourselves.

After people have composed their list, I ask them to create an environment that's calming, centering, and peaceful. I want them to find somewhere specifically for this exercise, whether in their home or elsewhere. They can use incense, candles, music, a bath, or anything that works for them.

Once this space is set up, I ask the individual to take their one hundred acknowledgments, together with a childhood photo of themselves between the ages of three and five, and bask in their greatness until they get present to who they truly are. I want them not just to recognize their acknowledgments, but to really feel themselves present in these acknowledgments.

Because I believe in the magnificence of all humans, even those who society deems monsters, people challenge me: "How can a murderer be great? How can someone like Hitler be great?"

The simple fact is that Hitler did what he did because in the course of his upbringing he lost all awareness of the person he was born to be, as is the case with anyone who commits a terrible act against their fellow humans. When we lose touch with our essence, any one of us can do horrendous things.

How easily our greatness becomes buried can be seen from my experience over an eight-year period during which I tried to transform the way New Zealand goes about youth reform. When I began this work, there was no reform process either pre-prison or post-prison. Can you imagine? Not a single effective program sought to circumvent the vicious cycle of recidivism. In the course of this work, we unearthed an alarming statistic: 65% of youth within the prison system had a condition known as "glue ear." With this condition, the person not only can't hear clearly, they have difficulty processing the limited information they do hear.

These individuals were habitually labeled "dumb," "inadequate," and "stupid," yet the condition has nothing to do with the quality of the person's brain. They were individuals who wanted to have a role in society—to belong in their school, among friends, and in their family—but life let them down. As a result, their only way to gain attention, which all children need, was to do so in ways that were dysfunctional. In those days, such behavior led them down a one-way path to prison. Because no one recognized or celebrated their greatness, least of all themselves, there was no attempt at reform. They were simply locked behind bars.

Glue ear is but one example of those syndromes that rob children of awareness of their greatness as we increasingly brand them "Asperger's," "autistic," "attention deficit," and so on. I believe all these labels limit children. By labeling them in this way, we're actually *setting them up* to lead a dysfunctional life.

The labels imposed on these children come with no support for the parents who have to deal with their children's challenging behavior. I've met so many parents who feel totally alone and utterly helpless as they seek to do their best for their child. Such parents sought advice from the medical and counseling professions, but instead they received labels rather than assistance in coping with what they were dealing with. In other words, because there was a complete lack of understanding of the root of the issue, the approach taken was to brand

and sedate the child, ruining the child's ability to express its creativity in a meaningful form.

Sedating our most creative children isn't a solution. I believe it's our responsibility as a human race to find real solutions. I feel for parents who have to cope with a child who stretches them beyond their coping skills. Despite expending a great deal of time, money, and energy on trying to help their child, they find themselves at their wits' end. A label solves nothing!

My experience has taught me there's another way. Professionals shouldn't listen to children for their *label*. They should listen to them for their *greatness*.

When children are listened to for their greatness, they respond marvelously because they have never before been in the presence of someone who acknowledges them for who they really are. This, by the way, is true of every person I coach. They have never been listened to for their greatness and consequently can't recognize greatness in themselves.

moving into self-validation

Now comes the truly self-confronting aspect of this exercise. Again and again, when we come to this part, clients say to me, "Why on earth do I need to do this?"

I ask clients to share their list of acknowledgments with three people with whom they would find it challenging to share what they have written. The individuals selected for this are each asked to read the acknowledgments quietly to themself, then offer feedback.

During the feedback, I ask clients not to focus on the other person's response, only on their reaction to what the person says. This is because we can learn a great deal about ourselves by witnessing how others respond to our acknowledgment of ourselves. If we find we are unable to be with what the person says without either reacting to them or recoiling from them, we're seeing an area in which we haven't yet truly acknowledged ourselves. This is the place we need to go to work.

Let me share with you some of the standard responses people tend to receive. Mothers often want to critique the spelling, God love them. This is because they are unable to be present with what's being shared. Fathers are so unable to be with what's shared that they feel a need to change the subject. Children want to rush off and do the exercise themselves—they love it! And then there are those who are so blown away by the depth of the person's sharing that they acknowledge them in a way they have never acknowledged them before.

when another person can no longer devastate you

A client who was thirty-four years old had experienced a lifetime of difficulty with her father. She disliked him, finding him to be a cruel man who had been abusive to her most of her life. He never approved of her and finally disowned her, yet she never understood why and longed to change the situation.

This woman decided to share her list of acknowledgments with her father. Can you imagine what an internal struggle this was for her? Nevertheless, given her commitment to integrate her perceived issues with her father, she confronted her fear and waded right in.

The result? After her father read her acknowledgments, he remarked, "That's rather conceited, isn't it?" Then he walked away.

As this woman asked herself how her father could be so cruel in the face of such openness, she experienced the breakthrough she required. She realized that, all her life, her father had known she sought his approval, yet he had deliberately withheld it. In the act of sharing her acknowledgments, at the height of her vulnerability, she got it big time that although she had been making it all about her, it wasn't about her!

For thirty years, she had been giving her father's cruelty a meaning it didn't have—that there was something inadequate about her that caused him to withhold. Now at last she knew it wasn't about her at all.

Because she had made herself so vulnerable, to receive such a response left her with no way forward other than to completely let go of her issues around her father. In the letting go, he lost all power over how she felt about herself, and in that moment she regained her power.

It's crucial to realize that if an individual responds negatively, it's never about us, only about them. Once we are able to validate ourselves with our own acknowledgment alone, without the need of external validation, nothing that happens in our life will cause us either to react negatively or recoil. Instead, we embrace situations exactly as they are.

The phase of this exercise we've just covered isn't for the fainthearted. It's for those who, after perhaps years of pain, are willing to reclaim their power in a way they have never experienced and reap the rewards.

This exercise is so powerful, it has reunited couples even after divorce. It has resolved dysfunctional family issues with children and stepchildren. It has healed many relationships between siblings and parents, in some cases where there's been no communication for years.

It has given people a sense of coming "home" to themselves.

If we are unable to acknowledge ourselves for what we have achieved to date, there's nothing moving forward that will register on the radar. We are so hell-bent on scoring achievements, but for what purpose? What's the point if we aren't present to what it is we have achieved? I joke with my clients that they are lucky I don't ask for a thousand acknowledgements.

When we can be devastated by what someone says or does, it means we're still operating from our default identity. When we come home to ourselves, we're no longer impacted by external circumstances. We have entered into our power and are able to appreciate our magnificence.

Chapter 9

c o n s c i o u s n e s s
c r e a t e s   c o m m i t m e n t

Most of us say we want to experience transformation. However, there's a huge gulf between *wanting* something and being *committed* to it.

Humans operate from three different levels. Understanding these levels helps us recognize what holds us back from the commitment that can transform our lives.

At level one, we say we "want" transformation but do nothing to bring it about. In other words, our search has no integrity and hence we don't receive the results we say we so very much desire. When we do nothing yet expect results, it's because we hope what we wish for will magically "appear" someday—that our circumstances will somehow wondrously improve, making our life better.

The key element that drives this inactive approach is a belief that in effect states, "You can't do what it is you want to do because you have to wait on fate. If it's meant to be, it will be. If it doesn't happen, it wasn't meant to be." When such a belief is running the show, we are essentially paralyzed.

At level two, we involve ourselves in a measure of activity. Such activity is evidence of at least a degree of integrity, since we actually do something about what we say we're committed to. Because we are confronting some of the beliefs we hold with regard to going for what we want, we obtain results—albeit not everything we desire.

When we fail to embrace everything the infinite Presence is asking us to do and instead do only a limited version of the activity required to achieve what we want, we can only ever produce a limited version of what this Presence wants us to have—an end result that's always inferior to what we could have. How do we know the infinite Presence wants us to have the full version of what we say we are committed to? Because this Presence gave us the desire in the first place.

If we seek to sow little and reap much—to garner rewards without the work—then what we are *doing* isn't *being*. Our activity isn't an expression of who we are. Work has to be an expression of our love of life, not merely a means to make money so we can eventually stop expressing our creativity and drink cocktails around the swimming pool. How else can we be co-creators? Co-creation isn't something we do for a time in order to retire—the sooner, the better. To co-create is our *nature* and our eternal destiny, not a temporary necessity to keep body and soul together.

Many of us bring an unsupportive if not highly critical attitude to our work. To become a co-creator is to stop undercutting each other and support each other by bringing our best to every endeavor. This means we get out of the right-and-wrong mode. Oh, we may think someone is wrong or that they should have done something differently. But so what? It just is what it is. Nothing is achieved by going there. Instead, the way forward is to get excited about being in a creative mode. If we don't want to serve in a creative way—if we don't feel *honored* to serve—we ought to get the hell out of that industry.

In other words, it's a question of *believing* that the infinite Presence seeks to manifest its goodness through us. The desire we experience *is* this Presence desiring through us, wanting to express its loving nature. To the degree we entrust ourselves to what our heart longs for—what we sense we are here for—we move into action in line with these desires.

Of course, I'm talking about the deep desires of the heart. But even those passing whims we sometimes mistake for our real desires will, although perhaps painfully, lead us to recognize what it is we actually want. Dead end paths are just a roundabout way of finding our way to consciousness.

At a conscious level of living, we no longer deal in limited results because we do everything a situation asks of us. However, when I say we "do" everything, I mean something fundamentally different from manipulating, controlling, and forcing our way through life, which is what so many equate with "doing."

While conscious doing is a highly active state, it's simultaneously a wholly surrendered state. It involves responding to what the universe is putting on our plate. We show up in those areas in which life is inviting us to show up and has equipped us to show up, rather than shoving our way into the spotlight out of our default egoic identity. At this level, because we have a high degree of integrity, we produce the results we really want.

In a nutshell, to achieve what we say we are committed to, we must identify whatever beliefs are *really* running the show in our life and face up to those beliefs that limit us.

the wimbledon model

The game of tennis is a helpful analogy for these three levels of commitment. In country-style tennis courts, the playing field is uneven, the lawn not mowed, the net full of holes, the balls of questionable quality. It's a low-level game.

There's a more professional court on which amateurs play. It's a quality facility, more prestigious, tailored to a mid-level game. And then there's Wimbledon, superior in every way—the ultimate tournament with worldwide exposure, elite status, where competitors play an extremely high-level match.

People who only *wish for* results operate from level one or two, whereas people who are *committed* to results operate from level three. They play at Wimbledon!

Where are you operating in your life in light of the analogy of playing at Wimbledon?

When I asked this question in one of my seminars, a person confessed, "My God, Sally, I'm not even in the grandstand watching! I'm in the parking lot." When we are in the parking lot of life, we are merely enduring. The reason we put up with this low level of functioning is that we are numb to our real desires and subsist on wishful thinking. Shut down to our authentic self, we are unaware of what it's costing us to content ourselves with merely "getting by" instead of embracing life wholeheartedly.

If we move out of the parking lot and into the stadium, at least we're aware of our desires. Sadly, though, this is where many of us remain for years. For instance, how many people do you know in your own circle who *think* and *talk* about what they want to do, yet who never fulfill their desires? They may have entered the stadium, but by merely sitting in the grandstand of life, they abdicate their responsibility to be on the court.

The game of life can only be won *on the court,* and as far as I'm concerned there's only one court in life and that's Wimbledon.

To live life at level three is tremendously confronting, and consequently most of us get off the court when the confrontation seems to stretch us too far. But the tennis pro who is being watched by millions doesn't walk off the court when being confronted. Whatever shot comes their way, they step right up to it. Indeed, a person playing at Wimbledon *lives* to be confronted—it's the nature of the game. When the ball is coming at them at 120 miles per hour, the high velocity produces superior results because the tennis pro continually "dies" to themselves as the player they presently know themselves to be so they can rise to a higher level of performance.

To play at the Wimbledon level in our everyday existence, we need to embrace being confronted as a way of life. In fact, we have to go looking for situations that stretch us. Unless we fall in love with being stretched, we can't expect to transform anything. However, when we embrace confrontation consistently, those situations that at first frighten the life out of us become our new comfort zone.

How many people do you know who have gone for what they want, found themselves confronted by an obstacle, and ended up getting off the court because they were afraid? The reality is most people get off the court when they are confronted. This is why I train people to stay on the court and confront *themselves,* which a person does by facing up to whatever level of default emotion is surfacing in them. Self-confrontation is the key to experiencing transformation. Indeed, it's the *access point* to transformation. By confronting our default emotions, which only survive because we feed them, we terminate their ability to undermine our commitment.

When we engage in highly conscious activity and are unfailing in holding out for the result we truly want, we show we are committed to manifesting our true being no matter what. Then the consciousness that undergirds the universe, and which invited us into existence in order that we might show up, lines up behind us in all its power.

how we become stuck

Are there things in your life you would like to stop doing? Are there things in your life you would like to start doing? Are there things in your life you would like to do less of and things you would like to do more of?

Many of us can't answer these questions with conviction because we're stuck in the "how" of what we would like to happen. We ask ourselves: How can I stop working at a particular job when I don't have the money? How can I start doing a particular activity when I don't have the time? We don't give ourselves permission to seriously consider what we'd like to change because to become focused on the "how" is the death knell of all possibility.

How convenient to be stuck in the "how!" If we believe we have to know how something could come about before we move on it, then it's not likely to happen. "How" keeps us in a state of confusion, which immobilizes us. As long as we don't know how, we won't have to show up in our life. We won't have to rise to the challenge of our greatness. A world in which people no longer hurt will remain a seeming impossibility.

To be in a state of confusion is nothing more than to be knotted up in our projections, which allow us to use the "how" as what I call a relinquishment bucket. Again and again, I hear people reason: But how can I find someone to marry when I've been single for so long? How can I leave my job and go for what I really want when I don't have the money? How can I leave my marriage, even if it is miserable, when we have four children together? How can I take time out for a vacation when I have so much debt? The relinquishment bucket is bottomless.

When we no longer toss our desires into the relinquishment bucket and we ban the throwaway word "how," focusing instead on forwarding our game rather than on *how* to forward it, the way forward unfolds right on schedule. In other words, the "how" sorts itself out once we are clear about our direction and move into action. The old cliché applies: "When we move, providence moves too."

it's not about money or time

We all have a variety of reasons we don't go for what we say we want. Money and time are two of the principal reasons, though both are actually excuses. Whatever we complain about is never the real issue. The issue we're complaining about is always a symptom, not the cause.

For example, when we use lack of money as an excuse for not going for what we want, it's not about money. When I hear someone complain that money is their issue, I know it has everything to do with their *self-worth*.

Similarly, that other popular relinquishment bucket—busyness and lack of time—is just a way to avoid connecting with our feelings. When people complain they don't have enough time, it's always a function of their *fear of connection*. If we actually took time out and weren't busy, we would have to feel. When we are disconnected from our true self, this is something we avoid at all costs.

The ultimate phase of the consciousness journey is to experience such a level of integration that we become creative expressions of our Source—in other words, integrated manifestations of the divine. This is the destiny of every human ever born. It's a journey there's no avoiding, a path each of us must eventually tread.

There's no one who can't play the game of life the Wimbledon way.

Chapter 10

what to do when
you get stuck

Have you found yourself making progress for a while, then falling back? Whether in our personal life, a relationship, or our career, many of us find we do well for a time but can't sustain the growth we thought we had achieved.

I believe a key reason individuals and organizations invest a lot of money in personal development and change programs, yet few experience lasting change, is that insufficient emphasis is placed on sustainability.

The key to sustainability is how in touch we are with the present moment. Most of us have little idea how dissociated we are from the now.

Enduring satisfaction doesn't come from achieving a goal for which we've striven and driven ourselves, imagining that when we "arrive" at our goal we will be fulfilled. It comes only from enjoying each moment as it unfolds.

To experience fulfillment, we must anchor ourselves in the now. As long as we look to the future in the hope of achieving fulfillment, we are bound to experience a letdown—a feeling of, "Is this it?" We'll be disappointed and likely give up.

When we are anchored in the now, our creativity becomes an expression of the fullness available to us in the present moment instead of a means of achieving fulfillment sometime in the future. This approach stresses who we are *being* in the present moment.

For this reason, my coaching is *heart-based* and *internally focused,* which brings people into the present moment. I'm interested in shifting us into a *feeling* state. Unlike an emotional reaction, which is based on a past experience or a fear involving the future, shifting people experientially is where the key to sustainability lies.

a mode of being

Standard coaching focuses predominantly on areas of our lives we wish to transform, whether in our personal or professional lives. Coaches tend to emphasize there's a lot to "do" in our business or personal life if we are to get to where we want to be.

I perceive this process to be quite head-based, analytical, and what I call "prescribed," versus heart-based and intuitive. I believe there's far more to coaching than this project-management approach. Most people already have a very long list of things to "do" in their life, so the last thing I want to do is add to that list to then send them into even more overwhelm!

This is why I coach in a holistic manner, which means that whereas most coaches focus on the domain the client perceives isn't working, I focus on every area of the individual's life. I primarily want to know who people are *being*, not what they are *doing*. In fact, my focus is a hundred percent on the person's essential state.

Like other coaches, I help identify what a person wants to alter, except that I address the cause instead of the symptom. By resolving the cause, the particular domain in which the person is experiencing difficulty sorts itself out. Hence to transform a person's business, I focus on who the person is *being* in the business. Any action taken is done from a state of being, which is a completely different approach from taking action from a state of doing. After all, we're not human doings, we're human beings.

I believe the potential of the coaching industry to affect lives lies in leveraging what I term coaching in a co-creative way, which is limitless in its potential. Most coaches coach humanistically, which is limited coaching based in egoic strategies. They have yet to experience what it means to be a conduit.

Once we are no longer preoccupied with doing, we enter into what I call "culturalization." This is a state of being in which we enjoy a level of consciousness at which we *no longer need to attempt to sustain anything.* At this point, we have been enculturated into consciousness so that *being* has become our *mode.* Consequently, what we achieve in the way of transformation is sustainable.

two kinds of identity

We have seen that humans operate from two different states of identity. Our default state is to be disempowered, whereas our essential state is to be empowered. I teach people how to sustain living in their power-based authentic self.

To remain in our power, we have to be *clear what we want.* If we aren't clear, our default state will win because we'll give up on ourselves before culturization is achieved. In the face of the opposition of our own inner critic, let alone the opposition of others, we'll simply wilt. What's the point of achieving something if we have an inner critic beating the crap out of us to the point we are unable to sustain the change we're trying to make?

We also have to be ready to receive what we want. If we suddenly start getting what we want but are uncomfortable with it because it feels unfamiliar, we'll sabotage ourselves without even realizing we're doing so. Unless enough work is done on our default behavior, we'll forever undermine our efforts to achieve what we claim to want.

For transformation to happen, we must first recognize who we are being *right now.* We are each living at a certain level of consciousness, yet most of us are unaware of this level. In fact, most of us are so caught up in our default mindset, we have no clue a heightened level of consciousness is available to us. Metamorphosis can't get underway until we realize we are operating at a level of consciousness that restricts us to a limited experience of fulfillment. We must awaken to the fact we have a far greater potential than we are presently realizing.

Standard coaching practice sees coaching in terms of the present and the future with little if anything to do with the past. What has gone before is viewed as something catered for by psychotherapy or other forms of counseling.

Is the standard approach to coaching effective? Yes. Will you achieve your goals using this model? In all probability. Is it sustainable? Not in my opinion. This is why I don't adopt this approach.

If we are going to invest ourselves and our resources in transformation, we should make sure it's sustainable. I believe the key to sustaining change is to integrate the learning in an experiential fashion. Hence, I help individuals open up to a level of consciousness that will enable them to sustain change of their own accord without having to rely on any form of external system.

a call to consistency

There are times when someone is confronting their limiting beliefs, overcoming these beliefs, committed to what they say they are committed to, and taking all the right action, yet the results they want don't appear.

To understand why this happens, I draw upon an analogy from gardening. When we plant seeds, the plants don't grow instantaneously. Over time, as we nurture, cultivate, water, and fertilize, eventually we reap a harvest.

In China, there are farmers who plant a particular type of bamboo that requires six years in the ground before it even shows above the surface. That's a long gestation period. But without fail, overnight the entire plantation shoots ten-to-twelve-foot bamboo plants out of the ground. During the six years when nothing is visible, the farmers have to deal with not only their own doubts but also with the naysayers and disbelievers.

Just because results haven't yet shown up doesn't mean results won't be produced. If a venture to which we are committed is flowing from consciousness and we are doing the work that's necessary to fulfill our commitment, the results will come at the right time. Unfortunately, most of us give up at the eleventh hour just as the tables are about to turn.

I believe the only thing usurping people's ability to receive what they want is their belief that it isn't possible. This keeps them from doing what's required. When people consistently believe, their belief drives self-confrontation, which in turn generates commitment and action.

Again, let me emphasize that although there's action to be taken, work to be done, the actual emergence of the seed and growth of the plant requires no driving, striving, or forcing. In other words, we can't stand over a plant and say, "Come on, grow, you bastard!" If a plant is properly nurtured, it's going to grow in its own time without the aid of any anxiety on our part.

Moment by moment, we have a choice to live in either an empowered or disempowered state. If we are clear on our goals, clear on why we are here, have healed our childhood wounds, are complete with our parents, are cognizant that the key to freedom lies in responsibility, commitment, and integrity, and are present to the choices that are before us moment by moment, we can sustain living in an empowered state.

when the wheel comes off your wagon

Having said all of this, I want to offer one word of caution. From my experience with a great many clients as well as in my own life, a wheel sometimes falls off our wagon.

I teach people to simply acknowledge what has happened when a wheel falls off their wagon, have compassion for themselves in that moment, and put the wheel back on without drama. The key to mastery is the length of time it takes to put the wheel back on.

When the wagon wheel is off, I like to think of these as duvet days. We should expect to have duvet days; and when we experience one, we should have compassion for ourselves. We simply accept we are off center for the moment.

Why it's important to accept that our wagon wheel may fall off occasionally can be seen from the example of a diet. If we are on a diet and we binge for a day, some of us give up on the diet because we didn't follow through on what we were supposed to do. The key is to accept we will experience lapses. In fact, expect to experience such lapses! Few have ever gone on a diet and managed to religiously stick to the letter of the diet. So if you eat a packet of Twinkies, at least enjoy them! Most who eat the Twinkies beat themselves up even while they are eating them. Not only do they sabotage themselves, they allow their inner critic to make them miserable. To help deal with this, they have another Twinkie! This is ludicrous.

We are rarely told that when we have trained our cellular body memory to hold a certain weight or body fat percentage over a period of twenty or thirty years, it takes a minimum of nine to twelve months to change the cellular memory in a way that registers that this is the weight we are supposed to maintain now. We have cultivated our body to be a particular size and shape for decades, then we wonder why we aren't getting instant results! We have to train our cells to establish a new memory. So when we go hammer and tong at a diet for three months, which is about all most of us seem to manage, it's little wonder we give up when we don't maintain the weight loss we've achieved. To believe we could establish a new norm in three months is simply self-sabotage.

We invariably see it as "significant and serious" when we have "failed" at our diet, had a cigarette, or drunk too much. I look at such "failures" quite differently. I believe that to have the expectation that none of our wagon wheels are ever going to fall off is to sabotage ourselves before we even set out on our journey.

A key aspect of learning to live a life that's sustainable is total acceptance of ourselves at all times. Loving ourselves keeps us in the present moment, which enables us to continue transcending our limitations. Indeed, there is no limitation that can't be transformed by the love that flows whenever we're in the present moment.

Chapter 11

extraordinary
relationships

It's inconceivable that anyone would want to live in a world other than one of love. So why don't we experience such a world? The answer to this enigma will emerge as we explore human relationships, which are the arena in which love manifests.

What I'm about to share with you applies both to professional and personal relationships. It applies on the job, at the club, at our places of worship, and in the home. It applies to how we relate to our parents, children, in-laws, and relatives—and especially to how we relate in romantic relationships (for which I have some additional, specific insights to impart).

I believe there are four levels of relationship and only four. One is mere existence, two is just ordinary, three is good, and four is extraordinary. Each of these levels of relationship reflects our level of consciousness. No matter how "spiritual" we may imagine ourselves to be and no matter how good our talk, our relationships tell the truth about us. They mirror back to us exactly how conscious we really are.

If we are operating at either the mere existence or just ordinary levels of relationships, we are operating at a low level of consciousness. We are largely resigned to the way things are and consequently our commitment is low.

In such a relationship our focus is external. In other words, we think it's the other person's fault our relationship is the way it is. However, whenever we blame the other, we do so because we are *expecting the other person to make us happy.*

A good relationship, and especially an extraordinary relationship, is about living at a high level of consciousness with a high level of commitment to our own happiness. Instead of being resigned to a mediocre experience, we experience intense passion. The focus is internal, which means we don't look to our partner to make us happy. We recognize that our happiness is our self-responsibility.

relationships that merely exist

If we are in a relationship that functions at the level of mere existence, the name of the game is to dominate, manipulate, and control.

At this level, we believe everyone else is to blame for the fact we feel resigned and resentful. Feeling this way, we are completely judgmental of the other person and have no compassion for them. In fact, we intentionally try to hurt the other. We lie as a coping mechanism, a way of safeguarding our own insecurity.

When we operate from a state of resignation, we have no real desire to change the way our relationship is and therefore don't follow through on what we say we will do to bring about change. Because we don't take responsibility for our behavior, our focus is on making the other person wrong. And needless to say, we see everything as dramatic, serious, and significant.

In a personal relationship of a romantic kind that functions at the level of mere existence, there is either no sex or hardly ever any sex. We usually sleep in separate beds. And we may resort to sexually abusive behavior, such as seeking out a prostitute or having an affair.

In a relationship of mere existence, we have no sense of what a profound privilege it is to be in the presence of another human being. Consequently, we aren't present with each other. Because both of us are caught up in our own perceived issues, neither of us places a priority on the relationship. In fact, our behavior is destructive to the relationship. We are verbally, emotionally, sexually, and often physically abusive.

At the existence level of relationship, we operate primarily from IQ, coming from the head without heart. Our focus is entirely external, not at all on what's really going on inside us. We are simply oblivious of our true state, unaware we are locked into our default identity.

ordinary relationships

In an ordinary relationship, a lot of the same traits apply as in an existence level of relationship, with several additional factors coming into play.

Unlike in a mere existence level relationship, when we are in an ordinary relationship we generally want things to be better but we aren't committed to the change that's necessary. The reason we aren't committed is our fear of intimacy.

When there are no boundaries on what's acceptable or unacceptable behavior, it's because we believe we can't have our own voice in the relationship. We feel suppressed, as if we are losing ourselves in the relationship. The other person doesn't listen well to what we have to say, when we even have the courage to say it, and we are generally not a good listener ourselves. As a result, we either remove ourselves from communication or we express ourselves in the form of anger.

Though we are focused primarily on our own needs, we mostly live out of our victim identity, which means we feel powerless to change the situation. Focusing on what we perceive as issues, problems, and challenges keeps the drama in place.

If we are in a romantic relationship at this level, there is some sex but it's inconsistent. We are focused on gratifying ourselves, rather than on being present with our partner, or on "getting it over with" for the sake of the other. Romance is all but nonexistent. As with a mere existence relationship, individuals at this level of relationship also operate primarily from IQ, focused in the head and not the heart.

In such relationships, we are in our default identity. Consequently, one party's disempowered state triggers the other party's disempowered state. Neither of us is really present to the cost of this type of relationship. The result is that the relationship takes a low priority in our life.

good relationships

In a good relationship, our focus is on our internal experience. To be in touch with our inner being allows us to alter our behavior so it doesn't have a negative impact on others.

Because we have a genuine interest in the relationship, we honor the other person. As a result, we tend to be compassionate, wanting to enhance their well-being. We are also careful to follow through on what we say we will do, which means we can be counted on.

In such a relationship, we value boundaries and we take responsibility for our behavior. Because we don't blur the distinction between ourselves and the other person—don't project our take on things onto them—we appreciate the other as a quite separate individual. Consequently, we're in a place to be a good listener. Seeking to understand, as well as to express ourselves clearly so we are understood, our communication is genuine and powerful. Because we take the other seriously, really seeking to hear their heart, we are attuned to their desires. In fact, we genuinely care about wanting to bring them pleasure. We desire to work through any perceived issues because, in the main, we enjoy the relationship. Still, although we are committed, our commitment wavers at times.

In a romantic relationship, we want the relationship to be a first priority but have difficulty achieving this and tend to place it at a medium priority. Though romance is somewhat spasmodic, it's of value to both partners and we are open to understanding our partner's desires. There are good sexual relations, though they could be even better.

In a good relationship, we operate from EQ (emotional intelligence), which means we are primarily coming from the heart.

extraordinary relationships

An extraordinary relationship not only operates at a high level of consciousness, it evolves on an ongoing basis.

In such a relationship, we are nothing but compassionate to both ourselves and others. We realize what a privilege it is to be in the presence of another human being, so we are truly present with each other. We are passionate about life and have a sense of urgency.

In such a relationship, our focus is internal, centered, and calm. There are clear boundaries that have been established by the parties together. We're keenly aware that we are always responsible for our own emotional and mental state.

This means we take complete responsibility for our actions so that we never project our default behavior onto the other person. Indeed, we collapse all projections. Aware that relationship and commitment are a function of who two people are being moment by moment, we come from love all the time.

Because we are present, our communication is powerful. Our word is gospel, and whenever we communicate, we ensure our communication contributes to the other person in a positive way. We always listen to the other for their greatness, never for their weaknesses. We're so aware of who each of us truly is that we never mistake the other person's default behavior for who they are. Indeed, we listen to the other party in a highly receptive manner as one of our most valuable teachers.

The only kind of relationship worth having is one in which we are listened to as well as fully able to express ourselves. Can you imagine what it would be like to be really listened to in every aspect of our lives?

To listen and be listened to in this way is rare. I find that people have a default way of listening to each other that's automatic. We especially have an "automatic" way of listening to those closest to us such as our parents, children, friends, and spouse.

When I facilitate relationship coaching, I ask the wife what her default listening is of her husband. "He's useless," she might respond. Then I ask the husband about his default listening of his wife and he responds, "She's demanding." So when both parties come for coaching, I say to them, "Are useless and demanding having a good time?"

I then ask the same couple to spend one month coming only from love, being a contribution to each other, and listening to each other as magnificent. I also ask them not to communicate any time they are tempted to come from their default way of communicating.

Their response: "We might have an entire month in silence."

My response: "Get present to the cost of that."

When I make a recommendation to a couple to do this exercise, one of two things occurs. They commit to doing the exercise then go into avoidance and don't do it due to fear, or one party decides they don't wish to do the exercise. Does this not speak volumes for how disassociated people are to the cost of living in a default-based relationship? Anybody in their right mind would move in a heartbeat to be loved to the degree this exercise facilitates.

This affirms yet again that the results that show up in our lives are the product of what people are really committed to, regardless of what they say they are committed to. In my observation people are far more committed to keeping their dysfunction in place than they are to exploring the extraordinary. How sad is that?

In a romantic relationship, because we see sex as an integral form of communication—an art form that conveys a message—we have great sexual relations. Both individuals initiate and both are focused on mutual enjoyment. We see romance and spontaneity as essential elements of our relationship and we place a high priority on them.

I've worked with countless couples in relationship coaching who have difficulty with their sex life. I explain that sex isn't some "thing" they engage in, as if what they do in bed is detached from who they are as individuals and as a couple. It's an expression of their being and is a mirror of how present they are with each other. To have extraordinary sex is the result of a choice to relate to someone in a profoundly deep way moment by moment, so that the sex is a byproduct of who two people are *being* with each other.

your personal love language

He advocates that everybody has a primary love language. In an extraordinary relationship, we understand our partner's love language— that is, how the person receives and gives love. Then we communicate from this understanding.

When two people don't understand each other's love language, they experience a disconnect even when they are committed to each other. For instance, if our personal love language is physical touch and we are in a relationship with someone who doesn't tend to touch, unless we understand this, we aren't going to feel satisfied in the relationship.

Let me give you an example of what I'm talking about. In a seminar I attended in Melbourne during my course junkie days, the leader shared a story about his wife. For months preceding her birthday, he went out of his way to orchestrate the most amazing day without her knowing. The day began with a gondola ride down the Yarra River, complete with a champagne breakfast accompanied by opera. At lunchtime, they arrived at a restaurant where twelve of her closest friends had gathered. Following lunch, they were picked up by a limousine and taken to an afternoon performance of the musical *Les Misérables*. She was then escorted to a hotel suite, where there were canapés and champagne, together with ten more of her friends. Next, two handsome men escorted her to a separate hotel room where a beautiful evening gown sprinkled with rose petals was laid out on the bed with lingerie and shoes to match. After she dressed, she met her husband outside the hotel, where a Hummer limousine pulled up with twenty-two of her friends and they went to the number one signature restaurant in Melbourne. The evening concluded with phenomenal lovemaking.

The next morning, a change of clothes was on hand, another limousine arrived, and the couple went for breakfast in the rose garden, where two of their children were seated at a table awaiting them. During the breakfast, the man's wife leaned over to her husband and whispered, "But do you really love me?"

Amazed, he responded, "What does a man have to do?"

In terms of her love language, this woman required and used words of affirmation, whereas her husband's primary love language was acts of service, with gifts of service his second language.

The concept of love languages was born from a book entitled *Love Languages*, by Gary Chapman. For those committed to understanding their partner's needs, I highly recommend this read.

power-based relating

Of the four kinds of relationships we've surveyed, the only one that's a power-to-power relationship is the extraordinary kind.

An extraordinary relationship manifests three levels of intelligence. First it manifests SQ, which is spiritual intelligence. This is where we are connected to our inherent purpose. Next is WQ, wholistic intelligence, which is where we are profoundly connected to others and the collective consciousness. The ultimate is AQ, alchemical intelligence, which is the experience of being connected to everything we have the potential to be.

I say to couples, "What else is there other than being in an extraordinary relationship? Why would anyone want to be in something less?"

Let me summarize what we're talking about when I speak of an extraordinary relationship. We're talking about coming only from love, being a contribution, listening to the other person for their magnificence, and managing anything of a default nature separately from who the person truly is until they dissolve it.

Wherever there's a human-to-human interaction, whether in the home, on the factory floor, or in the boardroom, people function with each other in a manner that triggers their negativity toward each other. But it's only due to a lack of awareness of what this is costing us that the cycle continues.

Imagine a world in which every human interaction is only empowering! This, I believe, is possible when people take responsibility for living in an unconditionally loving manner.

When we think about human nature, we certainly don't frame it as a profound privilege to be human. It's not the way we view ourselves and it's not the way we view each other. If it were, each of us would have the opportunity to unleash our full creativity and have it valued.

The disconnect we presently experience from each other is so great that we can't even conceive of a connected world. Part of what I train people to do is to face the fear that stands in the way of becoming this connected.

the extraordinary relationship exercise

I invite you and anyone you are committed to having an extraordinary relationship with to engage in an exercise that can kick-start the journey into such a relationship.

To do this exercise, find a location where you can lock yourselves away for at least two and preferably four hours, somewhere you can't be disturbed. Agree that, after this time together, you are both committed to walking away with a game plan for what it means to be in an extraordinary relationship. Agree also you won't leave until you're both on the same page. Since fun is mandatory, set it up as a game, not a trial.

For the exercise itself, each of you think about the following questions and write down your answers. It's important to do this stage of the exercise individually. Here are the questions:

1. What's working in this relationship?

2. What isn't working?

3. What does an extraordinary relationship look like to me? (Be specific about what you would like *your* relationship to be like—don't answer in concepts and generalities.)

4. What do I feel I have to give up in order to have what I want in this relationship? (Note: some people feel they have to give up certain things for some reason.)

5. What do I feel is missing in this relationship?

6. What desires do I have that aren't being met in this relationship?

7. Am I willing to compromise what I want? If not, why not? And if so, what specifically? (Note: some people feel as though they need to compromise themselves or various aspects of their life.)

8. What stands in my way, keeping me from an extraordinary relationship at this moment? (For example, resignation or resentment.)

9. Am I prepared to show up like never before so this relationship can rock beyond comprehension? (Just notice if your answer is no; and if so, why. If your answer is yes, what might it feel like to show up in this way?)

10. Am I prepared to listen to both of us for our greatness? If not, why not?

11. Declare any thoughts, actions, or behaviors you engage in that don't come from integrity. (NB: This is an amnesty opportunity. No one gets to judge what's shared. It's an opportunity to just get straight about,

complete on, and clear of what's been in the way, and what until now you have been unable to articulate for fear of how it would land for the other party.)

12. What are the rules of engagement for moving forward? (For example: I will always communicate when I am tempted to withdraw and go missing in action. I will always clean up and apologize if I've been out of line. I will always manage my default behavior and not take it out on you.)

13. "I want to acknowledge you for..." Name ten things.

Once you've answered the above set of questions, come back together and compare notes. Take care to communicate from your power, not from your default identity. Get straight with yourself and each other more than you have ever been, which means being absolutely honest. Find where the holes are and come to an agreement on a game plan you'll put in place to reach a final agreement on everything. Then implement the game plan and have fun doing it.

When people do this exercise, they tend to get triggered by what their partner shares. For example, a wife writes twenty-three pages, while her husband writes two. Immediately, the husband gets triggered because he feels she's picking on him. I explain to the husband that when his wife writes more, it says more about her than it does about him.

Did you catch what I just said? This is an absolutely crucial insight that, once we fully embrace it, can transform the quality of a relationship. Let me state it again: when we're critical of another person, it says more about us than it does about the other person.

After completing this exercise, we need to be aware that, given the history of problems we have experienced, we may be unwilling to come only from love, be a contribution, and listen to each other for our greatness. If this is so, then we should get straight that we aren't committed to being in an extraordinary relationship. In which case, it's time to stop fooling ourselves and each other, wasting both our own time and that of the other person.

If anyone has difficulty implementing and sustaining the results guaranteed by this process, it will be for one or more of three reasons:

1. They choose to do their interpretation of the process, thereby obtaining their version of results.

2. They haven't clearly articulated boundaries on what's acceptable or unacceptable behavior.

3. They are giving lip service to the process versus applying it wholeheartedly based on their commitment to experience an extraordinary relationship.

As others before me have pointed out, intimacy implies we allow someone to see into us—"into me see." However, before we can see into another, we must first see into ourselves: "into *me* see."

Part of the reason we don't allow ourselves to experience people really intimately is that we're literally terrified of connecting this deeply with someone because *we've never connected with ourselves this deeply.*

When the context in which we communicate with another human being is entirely one of love, it can be extremely unnerving. When we come only from love, our authenticity—our sheer realness and desire to connect heart-to-heart—undermines the entire way we have all conceived of ourselves.

If we allow it to do so, our own buried authenticity will confront us to the core, showing us how we've betrayed the person we are capable of being. Our default position is that we are unable to be with this level of authenticity because it's outside anything we've ever known.

I've talked with people who are totally threatened by my very being. Yet it isn't in fact my being that threatens them. It's that by acting as a mirror, I'm showing them what they've never faced up to in their own life: *that they are in their essence unconditional love.*

In our default identity, we're simply unable to be with our power, our insight, and our capacity for complete openness. This is why we act out with dysfunctional behavior.

Couples brave enough to adopt the extraordinary relationship exercise, who are truly willing to look at who both of them are in the relationship, say, "Who needs Viagra when we've got the process?"

let me introduce you to fred

I also recommend to those interested in being in an extraordinary relationship that they choose a word on which they can both agree, perhaps something silly such as "Fred," as a way of flagging when they sense the other has moved into their default identity.

Every time either party perceives the other to be in their default state, they use this silly word as a state interrupter. However, the fact that one party says "Fred" doesn't necessarily mean the other is in fact in such a default state, only that this is the perception of the one interrupting. In other words, calling in Fred implies no judgment of the other—no "I'm right and you're wrong." It simply asks both to explore their present state.

Given the agreement that's in place, when Fred is declared, both are required to back off and apply the detrigger process to discover what they have actually been triggered by. When individuals ascertain what's really going on, they realize that nothing we perceive as triggering us in the present moment has anything to do with the present. It's always something unhealed from childhood.

When a word like Fred is used in this way, it diffuses what would normally be a serious, significant, and dramatic moment, dissolving it in a humorous way. Once the individuals are each back in their power, they can then re-engage and discuss what happened from a calm state.

To illustrate, a wife says, "You didn't put the garbage out."

The husband, still in his power, picks up on his wife's accusatory tone and discerningly responds, "Fred." Both must then back off without questioning the other or arguing. The couple must be absolutely clear that no matter how great the emotional charge either may be feeling in that moment, there's to be no more dialogue until both declare they are calm, nonreactive, and not defensive.

That they stop right where they are in their tracks, with not a word added, has to be an ironclad, immovable boundary in the relationship, or Fred will just become another point for argument. In fact, the reason I suggest a word like Fred, instead of encouraging a couple to make a statement such as, "You're moving into your default identity right now," is because it's important for them to be able to catch themselves as they are being triggered and then laugh together at the ridiculousness of it.

When two people really become committed, they won't even need to say "Fred." But in the initial stages, while they are operating from their default identity, it can be helpful.

how to detrigger in a relationship

A couple I was coaching had been locked in a state of argument for two weeks, each furious with the other. My first question to them was, "What happened to make you this furious with each other?"

Both replied, almost in unison, "I don't know. It's an accumulation of things."

I kept prodding: "What was the 'what happened?'"

People love to stay in confusion, which fosters drama, rather than get to the nub of the problem. It took me thirty minutes to drill down to what started it all. It turned out the husband had put a casserole on what the wife considered the "wrong burner."

In that moment, they both looked at each other and laughed, which for most couples I coach is exactly what happens. They get to see the ludicrousness of their arguments. There's almost always something ridiculous at the root of arguments. When a couple can finally laugh at themselves, it interrupts the drama.

I worked with the wife in the husband's presence, taking her through the detriggering process. "You acknowledge that what started all of this was his placement of the saucepan on what in your worldview was the wrong burner," I said. She responded in the affirmative. So I asked, "What did you make that mean?"

"He never gets it right," she said, "even though I keep telling him. He's incompetent because he never really listens to me. I've put up with this for twenty years!"

"Can you see that *you* added that meaning?" I asked.

"Yes," she admitted.

I then asked her what she made it mean about herself, to which she responded, "I'm angry."

We saw earlier that the third stage of the detriggering process always involves something unhealed from childhood. So for a person to completely detrigger, they need to recognize where what they are dealing with sources in childhood.

I next asked, "Do you acknowledge you've remained triggered for two weeks?"

When she agreed she had, I inquired what she was getting out of being triggered. She said she was getting "nothing" out of it, which is of course the usual response people give at this stage in the process of detriggering.

My task was to help her distinguish the benefits. "Do you get to be right and make him wrong?" I asked.

"Yes."

"Do you get to be justified about your point of view?"

"Yes."

"Do you have to be responsible when you are in a triggered state?"

"No."

"Do you get to be a victim, feeling powerless to change the situation?"

At this point she said angrily, "What do you mean? He damn well keeps doing it!"

I asked again, "Do you feel powerless in that?"

"Yes."

"Do you get to dominate, manipulate, and control?"

"What do you mean?" she again demanded. People who are triggered always love to respond with confusion.

Again I asked, "Do you get to dominate, manipulate, and control? Because whenever there is drama going on, someone is dominating, someone is manipulating, and someone is controlling—always. Can you see that this is what you've been getting out of the situation for the past two weeks?"

In other words, I wanted her to see that being triggered was her attempt to "set her husband straight."

When she agreed I was on the mark, I ventured further: "What is being triggered costing you?"

On this she was immediately clear: "Peace, love, relatedness. It impacts my energy, my intimacy, my well-being." This woman could see that by operating with this kind of behavior, she had paid a high price.

I explained, "Now you are aware of what's happened, you have a choice. Do you now choose to be responsible, based on what it is you say you are committed to? You are either interested in an intimate, loving relationship with your husband, or you are committed to making him wrong. You get to choose."

So it is with all of us. The quality of our relationships is something we get to choose.

the marriage dilemma

For couples in my audiences who have been together for a long time but who have chosen not to get married, I put to them, "If your decision not to marry has nothing to do with your past, I will back off."

I've found that in almost every case, a couple's decision not to marry turns out to be related to their past. I explain to such couples that there's no potential for their current relationship to become fulfilling if a past-based paradigm is running the show.

In response, the couples usually argue, "But why do we need to get married?"

As I listen to a couple's words, I notice that their language and tone are charged. This clues me into the fact something more is going on than the words in themselves reveal. Both their tone and their argument are always defensive.

In my audiences, individuals have even gone to the point of projecting back onto me, "Who are you to challenge me in the area of relationship? Are you in a relationship? Have you had children?" Can you hear the defensiveness in this?

A person who isn't carrying a charge from the past isn't at all defensive. That's when I know a couple are complete with their past and comfortable with their relationship without marriage. It's not that I'm an advocate for marriage. I'm an advocate for shutting the back door to any past-based behavior that a couple carry into the present.

I first point out to a person who's defensive that I have no interest in challenging anybody and am only interested in helping people learn to be the loving individuals they really are. I next point out that I lived at the most painful end of human-to-human interactions for much of my life, so I recognize when people are in pain. I then walk up to the individual and say, "I will do whatever it takes to make a difference in the life of someone who is in that level of pain."

When people have a point of view they express with a negative tone that evokes their anger, it doesn't cause me to become defensive in return. I've learned that such anger can become the access point to changing our resonance, so that it becomes positive and thereby alters the outcome of the situation.

In coaching anyone, I see in them their greatness. Wherever humans relate, whatever the nature of the relationship, I see the potential for an extraordinary relationship.

Just as birds have a built-in desire and tendency to build nests, so also human beings have a built-in desire and tendency to build relationships. The challenge is to build relationships that are humane, that serve every individual involved, and that add to the creativity and diminish the suffering in our lives. It's within our reach to have extraordinary relationships.

friendship with special benefits

All interactions follow a standard process when conflict is present. This is because all conflict ultimately stems from an indictment of someone's values, which starts when an expectation isn't fulfilled. We can see how this proceeds in relationships, often in contrast to friendships, from the chart below:

RELATIONSHIP	FRIENDSHIP
An expectation is unfulfilled	We don't usually have unfulfilled expectations of our friends
We make the person wrong	We don't tend to make our friends wrong
Our communication becomes constrained	We don't often feel constrained in communication with our friends
Our love is conditional	We are quite unconditionally loving toward our friends
We amass evidence to back up the default way in which we listen to our partner	We tend to listen to our friends as great all the time
We question the person's commitment	We hardly ever question our commitments with our friends

I am generalizing when it comes to friendships. But that being said, we are usually far more accepting in our friendships. Let's examine the six steps in the chart:

- **Step 1** There is an unfulfilled expectation. When we experience conflict in the context of a relationship, nine times out of ten it starts with an unfulfilled expectation. The irony is that 99.9% of the time the other party doesn't know what the expectation was!

- **Step 2** As a result of the unfulfilled expectation, we automatically make our partner wrong.

- **Step 3** We now feel resentful, which causes us to constrain our communication, if not remove ourselves from all communication, which is how we begin to manipulate the situation.

- **Step 4** Love becomes conditional when expectations aren't met. Individuals feel it's their right at such times to withdraw their love.

- **Step 5** To substantiate having the back door open so we can make our getaway, we need to find evidence to keep our partner in the dog house. (This also works with such people as our colleagues at our places of employment.) Our ability to listen is seriously deficient at such times.

- **Step 6** As a result of our ability to justify keeping the back door open, we question our commitment to the relationship.

To circumvent the domino effect of the six stages in the chart, take time to reassess your expectations—to examine where you are coming from in whatever you ask for from your partner. If you wish to be empowered in the many different situations that arise in the context of a relationship, give up your expectations and re-presence yourself to the love that's your essence.

Given that the word relationship is freighted with past-based meaning that hinders people from experiencing their relationships as extraordinary, it's obvious that when we operate from a lower level of consciousness, our communication is inherently disempowered, whereas conscious communication is always empowered.

Here's something that may surprise you: we *always* know the difference.

Chapter 12

b e c o m e   y o u r   v i s i o n

Showing up in life means we show up for who *we* are as a unique individual, and we do so unapologetically.

As we find ourselves increasingly showing up, it becomes important to develop a vision, mission, purpose, and core values. Part of my work as a coach is to partner people as they unearth their vision, mission, purpose, and core values. Whether I'm working with an individual or a corporation, I explain that the vision is the *what,* the mission is the *how,* the purpose is the *why,* and the core values are the *operating state.*

To show up in our vision, mission, purpose, and core values requires responsibility, commitment, and integrity. To many of us, responsibility, commitment, and integrity feel restrictive. Because of experiences in the past in which we were forced to do something contrary to our will, we rebel against responsibility, are frightened of commitment, are squeamish when it comes to integrity, and have a slippery adherence to our core values. We don't realize these are the qualities that lead to true freedom.

the freedom to commit

What we *value* is the lynchpin of responsibility, commitment, and integrity because each of these flows from what we really care about.

Most of us know what we value, but we don't live true to our values. What's the point of knowing what we value unless we live those values? Hence I say to someone, "Don't list integrity as one of your values unless you are prepared to live a life of integrity. Don't list passion unless you are willing to show up 24/7 for your passion. Don't say love is what you value unless you are prepared to come from love in every interaction you have."

115

If we don't relate to these qualities as freeing, it's because we've been wounded. When we are wounded, responsibility sounds onerous to us, while commitment is like a prison sentence. In fact, many of us are so wounded in the area of commitment that we probably ought to change the marriage vows to read, "I do, moment by moment by moment," because this is all we can commit to! As for integrity, our word in so many cases means nothing. We lie but make it okay. We generalize but make it okay. We betray but make it okay. We tell people a half-truth to avoid discomfort, theirs or our own. In so many ways, we are inauthentic.

Usually people won't admit they're not responsible, not committed, and out of integrity. "What do you mean I'm not responsible?" they retaliate.

To transform anything, we have to own which aspect of us is currently running the show. If we can't own we are irresponsible, we certainly won't change our life. In contrast, realizing how we veer from what we say we value is an opportunity for us to reinvent ourselves.

The real issue with lack of money, lack of time, and our other excuses for not showing up in our life is that we refuse to take responsibility. This means we aren't dealing with how we feel inside. When we don't deal with our feelings, we can't be passionate about our life, which means we won't be clear what we are committed to and therefore won't commit.

The first task is to articulate what we want and don't want. This is something I ask people to do before they go anywhere near goal setting. This is because few really know what they want. Oh, they may say they have goals. But whenever I ask about their goals, I notice these goals tend to be aimed three, five, or ten years out. When goals are oriented to the future instead of to what we can embark on right now, what we say we want is only ever seen as a distant dream. The truth is we don't know what we truly want.

How can we possibly fulfill our purpose unless we're crystal clear what we are passionate about? And if we can't articulate what we want, how can we expect the universe to deliver?

If we don't know what we want, what we are motivated by, and what we are committed to, then of course we won't be passionate. For our true desires to emerge and real commitment to form, we have to get out of our head and into our heart. We take our mojo back only when we get clear what we are committed to.

I asked a client what he was passionate about. His response, said with real disgust: "I think passion is totally overrated!"

Most people will back off in the face of someone who is extremely defensive like this. I take the opposite approach. When we are in the presence of someone who is defensive, what they say and how they say it tells us everything we need to know if we are to help them find their power. One of my key roles as a coach is simply to partner people in experiencing reconnection with their authentic self. I believe a sign of a good coach is that the coach never answers a question. She or he simply facilitates a conversation that enables the individual to answer their own questions. If we don't muddy the waters with our advice but allow people to inquire, they discover their own answers each and every time!

None of us can sustain passion unless we are coming from our *power*—that is, unless we are motivated by *who we are*.

committed to not being committed

Remaining aware but not moving into full consciousness is the biggest relinquishment bucket. If we are confused and therefore not taking our mojo back, we are committed to *not* living consciously, no matter how much we claim to be consciousness seekers. In fact, we are just that: consciousness *seekers*, not finders.

As long as we are aware but not yet really conscious, we don't have to be responsible. From the perspective of our default identity, this is the way we like it. This is because we aren't present to what it's costing us. So we go to seminar after seminar, retreat after retreat, telling ourselves we don't know why we aren't getting the results we say we want.

When we say, "I don't know," it's because we're operating from our default identity. I believe we always know, but it takes a high level of consciousness to be responsible. When we are responsible, all the answers flow from within. So the next time you tell yourself, "I don't know," catch yourself and ascertain what you are avoiding.

Whenever I hear someone say they don't know what they are passionate about, I know they are terrified of showing up. To be afraid—let alone *terrified*—of showing up for the magnificent individuals we are is simply a lack of awareness that our essence is love: a love of ourselves, a love of life, and a love of each other. To experience ourselves as love is the source of passion and the heartbeat of commitment.

Every time I facilitate a conversation with someone who says they don't know what they want to do with their life, I respond, "How convenient. It means you don't have to show up in your life."

When we are aware, yet operate over the top of our knowing, it's like icing on a turd. I've sometimes told people they would be better to remain unconscious than to become aware and then not be sufficiently conscious to be responsible!

a vision driven by *being*

Not many people have a personal vision, which to me is akin to being in a boat that has no rudder. If we wish to reach our destination, the first phase is that it's critical we get clear about our vision. The second phase is to go out into the world and share this vision.

It's at this stage that our ego confronts us: "Who am I to be fulfilling such an expansive vision?" Given we have nothing that supports our vision except our own belief in it, we might feel like a fraud. Nevertheless, we share confidently despite our fear, and sometimes despite people who think we are being ridiculous.

This is where we enter the third phase, which is integration of evidence we are on the right path. As we continue sharing our vision, in due course we begin seeing evidence to support the vision and we integrate this into the vision.

This is quite different from operating as a *doer* in life. A doer's life is disconnected because it's built on the person's or the organization's isolated effort, quite apart from the conscious field that undergirds the whole of reality. Consequently, whenever we approach life from a mentality of doing, we experience struggle, stress, and a feeling of being overwhelmed. Life lived this way is hard, generating pressure, frustration, and anxiety—all of which lead to a loss of vitality and a lessening of freedom.

To find life hard, to feel we are in a state of constant struggle, and to experience overwhelm is to live in a set of egoic labels that are the common currency of the dissociated. Yet how many people do you know who are overwhelmed, stressed out, and have been "busy" for years?

This syndrome is of course rife in the executive community because this community doesn't operate at a feeling level, as we can readily see from the common expression "business is business." Individuals in the executive community have to work countless hours to "keep it all in place." You would be amazed at the number of executives who tell me how proud they are of the heinous hours they put into their job. Why on earth would anyone work fourteen, sixteen, even eighteen hours every day? For them it's like a medal of honor. When I point out that it's actually a medal of martyrdom, they are shocked. To own the ludicrousness of what they are doing, they would have to become present to what it's costing them.

In contrast, to operate from *being* fosters connection with the whole of reality. This is a state in which we experience flow, ease, and inner peace. We quit striving to "make something happen" and become compassionate toward ourselves. We're like a leaf on a river. Borne along by the flow, it never struggles to get where it's going. When it reaches an obstacle, it simply rises above the obstacle and keeps going.

This is what it's like to enter into what people call the "zone." We take the same workload and even add to it, but we do the activity from a state of being. There may be tremendous activity, but it's all coming from inner peace. We move from driving, striving, and forcing, into experiencing life as flow.

A friend who is a phenomenal masseuse used to massage many of my clients. Her approach wasn't the normal sort of remedial massage. She truly gave people an experience of what it's like to be back in their body. To this day, I can't acknowledge her enough for teaching me the power of being back in my physical frame after decades disassociated from it.

One particular day, we both had overfilled client schedules in offices adjacent to each other. At the end of the day, I asked her, "How do you manage that many clients in a day?

"How did you manage the number of clients you saw today?" she responded. Her exertion was with the body and mine with the mind, but both of us function as conduits for energy to flow through us, which is why at the end of the day neither of us was drained.

When we are in the zone, we also become a conduit to attract synchronistic opportunities. Because we resonate at a different level from people who are struggling to accomplish something, we don't have to take a lot of prescribed action to achieve a goal. Simply by resonating in alignment with our calling, we become a magnet, attracting to us what we need in order to manifest our goals. Everything we need for our goals to manifest simply comes to us. This is the real meaning of the law of attraction: not that we try to make things happen, but that our true being draws everything we require to us.

Integration of evidence we are on the right track follows in the wake of experiencing synchronicity. All sorts of synchronistic events now occur to enable us to accomplish feats that previously would have seemed impossible. For instance, we meet someone who says, "What you are onto is a great idea!" They in turn introduce us to people who can forward our game. We discover what it means to be integrated into the oneness of being, so that when *we* move, providence moves too. In other words, as we come to understand what it means to reintegrate with that which created us, we begin participating in co-creation.

To be in the zone 24/7 is a matter of choice based on what we say we are committed to. If at some point we find ourselves slipping back into default behavior, all we have to do is identify the behavior. When we do so, we enter into a heightened consciousness and can re-access the zone at will.

Operating in the zone, we *become* our vision. In a very real sense, *we* disappear! Our calling is far greater than who we could ever be in our egoic human existence, which is why we step into a co-creative way of being. The evidence that shows up in this phase is beyond anything we could ever have imagined. We become our own mentor and become our vision, which leads to the fulfillment of our unique legacy.

Chapter 13

n o w h e r e   e l s e   t o   g o

To determine the legacy we will leave to the world is the most profound conversation we can enter into. It's the question of *why* we are here—what we are meant to *do* as a result of our *being* here.

Most of us think of our legacy as something we leave behind when we die. I'm talking about what's programmed into our being—both our essence and our DNA—and the way it calls to us from the minute we wake up in the morning to the time we go to sleep at night.

Our legacy is what we are meant to be: the dream that's built into our spirit and our genes. This legacy calls us forth to be all we can be and it's bigger than we have ever imagined ourselves to be.

Let me be clear that to fulfill our calling isn't merely about what we accomplish, but about *who we become.* When we are in touch with who we are meant to become, we are then led in life. We know where to go intuitively.

In 2005, when I Googled Legacy Leadership, I wanted to find out who was at the leading edge of legacy leadership in the world. I found the Legacy Leadership Institute based in Vancouver, Canada, and over a period of twelve months formed a relationship with this institute. A year later, I found myself in Vancouver embarking on being trained in every aspect of their course curriculum: legacy for the corporate world, legacy for community, legacy for education, legacy for kids. It was amazing to be on the other side of the world immersing myself in this conversation! I was in my element. They in turn were intrigued by the woman from New Zealand who called herself a legacy coach

121

and had been operating her own legacy leadership curriculum for more than three years.

My vision is one of:

Impacting Future Generations Through The Fulfillment Of Global Legacies.

It has since undergone a metamorphosis, which I spell out below. My 20 year vision: I believe there will be a day when:

- Traditional leadership models evolve beyond the humanistic realm to that of the co-creative realm

- The coaching industry raises the bar on walking the talk versus talking the talk, and unprecedented authenticity is experienced in the coaching profession.

- Those called to the profession of coaching embrace 'healing' as an integral modality to assure the sustainable transformation of self and said clientele

- There is no longer a divide between indigenous cultures and the mainstream.

- Spirituality will no longer be viewed as "woo woo," and we at last experience a world in which connection is primary.

- Depression and suicide will no longer be either experienced or tolerated in our global society.

- Those in the counseling and psychotherapeutic professions will stand for being whole *themselves* before attempting to help others.

- Those in the counseling and psychotherapeutic professions adopt the principle of going toe-to-toe with their clients to unearth the true gold that exists in the rawness of unprecedented authenticity.

- The human psyche no longer experiences the inner critic, and we as a race experience living intuitively, which is our birthright.

- The consciousness of the human psyche evolves to the level that fear no longer exists and love is the primary emotion felt.

- Equanimity rules, and wars no longer exist to propel the wheels of monetary gain.

- We as a species take responsibility for how truly powerful we are and no longer have a need to manifest cancer and other illnesses to learn our contractual lessons.

- We no longer compete with our fellow humans in either business or our personal lives, but all learn the art of *co-opetition*, which is our natural state.

- Those who have the power on this planet (and they know who they are) *collaborate* beyond their ego to truly make a difference in the world so that future generations can benefit.

- The face of our education system as we know it will change, and the future of our education lies in the establishment of co-creative schools and co-creative universities—educational institutions that champion the human spirit and feed the human soul.

Can you imagine young children being mentored to distinguish why they are on the planet at the age of eight, nine, or ten, then being wholeheartedly encouraged to manifest their magnificently unique expression of the Source that brought them into being? Can you picture governments operating at a high level of consciousness with a style of leadership that facilitates everybody's expression of their legacy? I believe the only thing preventing this from becoming a reality is our collective belief that it isn't possible.

discovering my own legacy

In the early days of my coaching practice, I called a colleague in Melbourne, Australia, on a monthly basis to say, "Glenn, it's not working."

He always responded, "Sally, keep going!"

There were moments when I resented his pep talks. But I recognized the fundamental lesson in what I was experiencing, which was that there was nowhere else to go.

I had dreamed of going out on my own for years and there was no going back. I didn't understand why things were happening the way they were, but I knew there was something for me to learn. I got down on my knees time and again and pleaded, "Teach me, show me, guide me." Each time I asked for guidance, I was directed further along the path of the unknown.

Humans seek safety. Generally, we look for safety in bricks and mortar, a bank balance, a relationship, and a career. Even when nations go out to conquer other nations, the basic drive they are fulfilling—albeit at great risk to their personal safety—is increased security, either in the form of eliminating their enemies or amassing material wealth by plundering their victims.

We live in a box labeled "I know." Everything in our life is benchmarked against this level of knowing. Consequently, most of us even approach self-improvement programs strictly from what we already know. Our focus is on adding to the box of what's known. We perceive everything from inside this box, which is where we feel in control and therefore safe.

What would happen if we stepped outside our box? We would step into what I call "belief and behavior land." The reality is that we don't recognize the beliefs we hold and how they drive our behavior until we actually step into an unfamiliar situation that calls them to our attention.

We are creatures of habit, which means anything related to the unknown frightens us. I lived a frightened life for years. However, nowadays my only focus from morning till night is on what I don't know. Why? Because what I know is limited, whereas what I don't know is limitless.

In so many of our lives, the known has us. It holds us prisoner. However, living a life in which nothing *has* us is the wave of our future.

As an example of what can happen when we break free of our limiting beliefs, I was asked to coach a man who had been headhunted by three high level strategic companies. Of the three, the job he wanted was the one he thought he couldn't get because it was with one of the top banks in New Zealand and he had no banking experience. I expressed that my interest in coaching him was to enable him to go for the job he wanted, since I specialized in belief and behaviors.

I question you, dear reader: how many times have you sold out because you believed something wasn't possible?

This executive was up against candidates who had more than twenty years of experience in the world of finance. Two of the candidates were flown in from London, which felt highly intimidating to him. Part of what I taught him was that he didn't need to understand the dynamics of an industry. All he needed was to understand the human psyche.

My client went through ten interviews with the bank at which he really wanted to work. Given the delays between the ten interviews, he was pulled first in one direction and then in the other because the other two companies wanted him. "I've got to go with what's known not what's unknown," he reasoned.

I told him, "You either sell out because of a belief, or you stand up for what you want." He needed to take a leap of faith instead of taking the safe route.

The list was down to my client and only one other candidate by the time the day of the final interview with the board arrived. Regardless of all the evidence he had seen as he was going through the process, he still doubted he would net the job. I said, "Do you honestly think you're going in there to be interviewed by the board?"

He looked confused.

"You're going in there to interview the board as to whether they are people you choose to work with," I explained. "Are they up to your standard? Claim the space."

I asked him to call me after the interview. When he phoned, he sounded excited. "God, you are good," he said. "I got the job!"

I responded, "You did the work. Congratulations."

By the time he had been in the role for nine months, he had blown away every strategy the bank had ever conceived of, taking them to an entirely new dimension—all with no banking experience at all! Yet when I first met him, there was no way he would have landed this position.

I ask you again, dear reader: what could be possible in your life if you truly believed?

birthing our legacy

For anybody who has pioneered something new, the masses listen with resistance because they operate in the known world, whereas the pioneer is introducing the unknown.

It took me until age forty-three to own I am a pioneer. All pioneers have made some form of personal sacrifice for their calling. People like Gandhi, Nelson Mandela, and Martin Luther King, Jr. had to keep showing up at great personal cost before their message took hold. How many pioneers are there in the world who haven't found their voice yet?

I believe I'm alive today for the purpose of facilitating conversations in which people find their voice. It took me more than two decades to find mine. Do you know how rewarding it is to sleep at night, knowing that every conversation I facilitate has the ability to change the psyche of generations not yet born? It's one fantastic vocation. I am fulfilled because I was finally able to claim my legacy.

I love facilitating people in birthing their legacy, which flows out of finding our own voice. When I coach, I give people permission to claim their essence, which is their birthright. It amazes me that this so often turns out to be something they have always sensed.

Even though people sense what their legacy is to be, they have never had anybody believe it, usually including themselves! It has always seemed too far-fetched. But when they find their voice, they find themselves expressing what they have always intuited but have never been brave enough to articulate for fear of being ridiculed.

In my own life, I've often wondered why I didn't become a housewife with children. Somehow, I always sensed this wasn't for me. Why do I think the way I do? For instance, where did the concept of co-creative schools come from? Where did the idea of co-creative leadership in businesses and governments originate? Facilitating the establishment of co-creative organizations and bringing together the most influential people on the planet isn't the kind of conversation most people have with themselves.

Our legacy has to flow from our inner being. If we, in our individual ego, are trying to change the way the education system works or change the psyche of governments, forget it. Only when we co-create with the infinite consciousness that's our Source can we transform the world. This is why I train people to access their co-creative ability, which enables them to enter a realm in which their potential is limitless.

Society says to us: Who are you to fulfill such an outrageous vision? From the level of our default sense of reality, I would agree. But the point is to die as we have known ourselves so we can access our larger self and embrace our co-creative power. In this reality, I say: Who are you not?

So I ask you: What has come to you as an expression of your essence that's far greater than you ever feel you could accomplish? If you can see it, your vision can precipitate your belief in it. Once you believe it and commit to it, the reality will come about by osmosis.

how to discover your legacy

Having facilitated conversations to help people distinguish their vision, mission, purpose, and core values many times in a variety of organizations in the corporate world, I'm clear that it isn't about hanging a plaque engraved with vision and mission statements on a wall.

In my observation, corporate consultants tend to focus on the identification of vision and mission for an organization. I question this approach because what's the point of establishing a vision and a mission when you don't know your "why?" In other words, you don't know what motivates you.

The first place I go with both an individual and an organization is to ask: Why do you bother getting out of bed in the morning? What is your "why"? All of us need to be able to answer this before we get anywhere near having a vision and a mission.

Few of us seem to know what motivates us. As an example, I was listening to a conversation one of my trainee coaches was having with a stranger one day, discussing with her why, of all the personal development programs in the world, she aligned with mine. As part of the discussion, she asked this woman, "What are your top three perfumes?" There was no hesitation in the woman's response.

Then the trainee asked the woman, "What are your top three motivators in life, the things that move you at your core?" The woman was tongue-tired, with not a clue what to say.

The trainee pointed out we have no hesitation identifying the most inane, inconsequential things in life. Yet the thing that matters most of all—that which we are motivated by, which sustains an impassioned state—we can't articulate.

Ask a guy what his top three football teams are and you'll get an instant answer. But ask him what motivates him and nine times out of ten he has no idea beyond "money" or the vague concept of "to be a success."

We can get clear on perfume or football, but we can't get clear on why we are here and why we do what we do?

The trainee was able to help this woman identify the reason she enrolled in my program, which was that her focus was incongruent with the only thing that really mattered in her life.

To facilitate a conversation with an individual or group concerning what their purpose is involves asking what the three things are that motivate them. In facilitating this conversation, I have learned that what people articulate is always pitched at a very high level. In other words, it's an *intellectual* description of what motivates them. I help people move from a high intellectual level to the emotive level because motivation is about passion—about *feeling*.

In this process, I get to watch people become present, perhaps for the first time in their life, to the cost of what in their life they have been operating over the top of. Can you imagine what this is like with the CEO of a large organization who is perhaps even moved to tears because someone has given him permission to feel again?

Having facilitated this conversation more than a thousand times, I'm convinced the three core motivators that drive most human beings are love, passion, and freedom. I believe these are the three issues at the heart of the human psyche. In truth, they are the only things that matter.

avoidance tactics

Most coaching addresses the symptom, not the cause. It's an egoic style of coaching in which the benchmark for the coach's success is the success of the client. The coach gets to tell themselves, "I'm a great coach because I have so many clients who are succeeding." It's a teacher-pupil dynamic.

Whenever I coach someone who is a coach, I'm aware they have a certain "listening" of what coaching is supposed to be. They come from a set paradigm with a whole slew of expectations of what coaching is going to look like. Instead of subscribing to the usual paradigm, I coach intuitively, which makes me a dangerous person to talk to. As someone speaks, I listen to their language. Then, from an intuitive perspective, I know where to go with them. This is different from prescriptive coaching. It's especially helpful with cynical people. In a group setting, the cynics are the ones with the most pain.

The business world tends to have a lot of cynical people. For instance, suggest to hard-nosed business people that if we could come from love, if we could experience freedom, and if we could fully express our passion, we would create a fantastic business environment. People in business don't believe you can come from this premise. In fact, I've often been challenged in board meetings by very strong, left brained, egoic, unconscious executives who say to me, "Who do you think you are to make a difference when you don't understand my industry?"

"I don't need to understand your industry," I tell them. "I understand the human psyche at a human-to-human interactive level, and in every business environment there's a human-to-human interaction." I'm a causal coach, not a symptom coach, and in every organization the cause is always the angst in the human-to-human interaction. It's never in the symptomatic aspects of an industry.

Management wants to say, "This is happening and that is happening," pointing to specific things they believe to be a problem. By so doing, they are keeping the concern at an unconscious, intellectual, removed level. Then, when the symptom doesn't go away, they bring in another consultant or another training company. These are just avoidance tactics.

Another popular avoidance tactic is to redo the vision and mission statement. In eighteen years of senior consultancy, every single organization I have gone into is still trying to determine what their vision and mission is. This constant re-visioning abdicates their responsibility for showing up. If they spent time fulfilling their mission instead of distinguishing a thousand iterations of it, they might get somewhere.

Most organizations lead by "consensus management." They constantly ask: How do I enroll the group in a new vision?

As an outsider looking in, I have on so many occasions witnessed that to try to gain a consensus is an act of sabotage. It promotes confusion and dysfunction within the company culture, thereby usurping the mission.

I say to the leader, "What are the costs of gaining consensus buy-in? Depending on the length of time you have been *trying* to design your vision, don't you think this time would be better spent implementing your vision?"

For example, New Zealand is one of the most popular tourist destinations in the world, yet the public transport system in Auckland, the nation's most populous city, is atrocious. For decades local government has tried to gain consensus among the public. They've spent eons thinking about, talking about, and trying to agree on a plan. As long as they continue to go down the consensus route, the city will never have an effective transport system. The situation cries out for someone to make a decision.

I come from a change-management background and am perhaps one of the most highly trained change agents in New Zealand. Off the back of my international experience, I believe the only way change can occur is that somebody has to step up as a leader and say, "This is the way." They have to show up, take the flak, and know that in the face of no agreement, if they stand strong in their knowing, eventually the scales will tip. That's leadership. When leaders engage in consensus-style management, it's not leadership, it's selling out.

An effective leader doesn't look for consensus buy-in. An effective leader leads with no reservations. Out of who she or he *is* in their *being*, other people get it. There's no vagueness, no grey, no lack of clarity. The vision is crystal clear, and when people catch this clarity, they become involved.

I feel I have the insight that can enable people to stop hurting if they'll use it. What a concept—a world in which no one hurts any longer! I learned what I learned so that others in the future don't have to experience the pain I experienced. This is why I'm hugely passionate about imparting the tools of self-mastery.

imagine a compassionate world

Imagine a compassionate world. It would be a world in which people are no longer judged, period. Instead, they are encouraged to show up, especially in the potentially most creative area of our life—our work.

Most of us experience at least an extensive separation between our business and personal lives, if not a complete disconnect. To-date this has served society. But as the world shrinks, we must respond to the quickened pace of life. We are all being called to evolve to new levels of functioning. In the world that's now dawning, to keep the business and personal dimensions of life separate would be to remain unconscious. The integration of every aspect of our lives is our assurance of the catapulting of our businesses and those who work in them to levels of consciousness beyond our present comprehension.

When I talk about love and intimacy in the context of business, the automatic response is defensiveness. People actually laugh. "Get out of here!" they say in ridicule. "You're talking nonsense."

Fish stinks from the head down. If the leaders of an organization embraced the ethos of love and intimacy, the impact on both internal and external customers would be immense. Imagine a business in which love is the only premise for everything done in the company. All corruption would end. Everyone would have an equal part to play, just expressed through different roles. Love would become a way of life instead of a platitude to which we offer lip service. We would actually treat others the way we would like to be treated—including our customers and the environment, whose wellbeing we would have at heart. Business would no longer be just business.

Do you see what's happening when people ridicule the idea of love as the driving force of business? The default immediately annihilates the possibility of such a way of doing business because its identity is threatened.

Both the business and the political realms appear to be the domain of the super confident. But this "confidence" is just a mask that hides the fear on which both business and politics are based. The reality is that people are so fearful, they can't imagine how they could compete in the marketplace and make money if they functioned from compassion. Most organizations are so focused on the bottom line, manipulating situations to produce what they believe they need, they don't realize that if their focus were love, the bottom line would sort itself out.

Imagine a world in which the workplace and the corridors of power are no longer a place of distress for anyone. What could we accomplish if we had loving organizations and caring governments? What might we achieve if every person in an organization understood the power of compassion? What might we envision for our world if creative cooperation motivated us instead of fear-based competition?

If we truly cared about all of our people throughout the entire hierarchical structure of business and government, there would be an end to the manipulating, gossip, rivalry, and backstabbing that zaps our creativity and comes only from fear. Work would to be a joy for everyone—something we all love participating in, rather than something we dread, feel forced to do, and regard mostly as drudgery.

Can you imagine being in a relationship, whether at work or at home, in which we're no longer afraid of what the other thinks of us? We wouldn't be worried about what our supervisor thinks of us, what our parents or children might have to say about something we do, or how our spouse might respond to our words and actions. Neither would we be anxious about whether our employer might lay us off, our family reject us, or our spouse have an affair or even leave us.

In every aspect of our life, we would be at peace, embracing everything as part of our ongoing journey into an expanding consciousness and the creativity that accompanies such consciousness.

surrender to your future

To sustain our evolution to higher realms of transformation requires us to surrender our identity to a higher calling than any of our societies across the globe currently recognize.

An example of this is my eight-year experience with youth reform. I founded and became committed to a trust called Future Youth New Zealand Trust. Of all of the philanthropic causes in which I could get involved, why would I align myself with the most damaged, hard-core youth of society? I wanted so badly to have a part in stopping the vicious cycle of recidivism. In fact, I became obsessed with a need to make a difference in the lives of the stereotypic youth who had the potential to perpetrate crimes such as I experienced.

In my effort to raise money for Future Youth, I met with anyone who would hear me. I even met with the head of the Mongrel Mob. Now that's extraordinary! After all, gangs have money. Many asked me how I got to meet some of the people I did. Well, I just picked up the phone and asked. For eight years, not one person with whom I spoke disagreed with the need for the youth programs I was advocating. But they weren't prepared to stand up and be counted, and I allowed a lack of follow-through because I was so "appropriate" in standing for my vision. It's taken many years since then to learn the art of not being appropriate in relation to fulfillment of a vision.

When I went to the United States and the Netherlands, I handed over the leadership. The Trust lost momentum. When I returned, I saw I couldn't sustain the level of commitment required in a society that simply wasn't committed to dealing with recidivism and youth reform. Part of the reason I closed Future Youth was to honor my commitment to the cause. I decided I would come back at a later stage when I was far more grounded, with my own backyard sorted out. People who have achieved a great vision say it takes ten years to fulfill on a vision of the kind I embraced. I learned the hard way what it takes—and why most people don't do it.

The world's societies focus on mind-oriented teachings. A world in which we no longer manifest adversity in order to learn would be an unrecognizable world. If we don't evolve our consciousness to higher realms, we will continue to manifest that which we always have. It's a heart issue that demands surrender. Surrender requires us to relax into the power of *trust*. This has nothing to do with relinquishing personal power. Surrender is relinquishing *control* in order to find our *power*.

Today, when a coaching client is ready to abandon their dream after being told "no" three times, my standard response is: "Do you know how many times I was told 'no' in the six years I worked in youth reform for Future Youth? 'No' is actually fuel for the fire. I learned that 'no' is a motivator." We need to claim the space internally by responding: "Do you know who you are talking to?'" When we own our presence, there's a new game in town!

a co-creative summit

My 20 year vision came to me in a meditation in October 2010. The culmination of this vision would involve holding the most powerful co-creative summit we have ever seen in the world, in Blanket Bay in Queenstown, a prestigious hotel in the South Island of New Zealand. As an aside, the brand of this hotel is a feather, which will become significant to you when you read my final chapter. I liken Queenstown to Sedona in the USA, a spiritual place. Most people who call themselves co-creators meet around a boardroom and talk. I am being called to summon *those who have the power on this planet, and they know who they are,* to congregate in Queenstown, New Zealand, to experience the first co-creative summit of its kind in silence. We need to *learn to be led* as leaders in the 21st century. I believe I have been prepared for all my life to facilitate a forum of this magnitude.

Ultimately, all rivers flow into a single global ocean. In a similar way, every single person on this planet has a legacy to fulfill that, if each of us does our part, will bring about the achievement of humanity's legacy: a world of love in which there is joy, peace, and fulfillment for everyone.

Don't tell me it can't be done. Don't tell yourself it can't be done. If we are to survive as a species, we must all surrender to this legacy. There *is* no alternative. We simply have no other place to go.

Chapter 14

spiritual discipline

When a client isn't operating at their full potential, I facilitate a conversation around self-discipline. It's the first place I go. If we aren't disciplined, our life will inevitably be out of whack. When we are disciplined, our life comes together.

People get up in the morning and go *do* their day. Many of us are overwhelmed by our to-do list. We push and rush to get everything done, imagining this is leading a "disciplined life." In reality, it's quite the opposite of a disciplined life.

Discipline in life begins with *spiritual* self-discipline.

In modern jets, passengers are instructed that if oxygen masks drop from the ceiling of the aircraft, each should put on their own mask before attempting to assist someone else with theirs. It's crucial to put the oxygen mask on ourselves before we try to help others or we'll pass out and be of no use to anyone. If we apply this analogy to our everyday lives, most of us are so busy putting oxygen masks on everybody else that we forget our own oxygen supply.

Or think of your life in terms of your car. Have you ever tried to get into your car and go somewhere when it has no gasoline in the tank? If we haven't fueled the car, it can't go anywhere, and it certainly can't go the distance.

It's no different in terms of our to-do lists. If we're so busy *doing* that we don't take care of ourselves, how can we expect to get where we want to go? We stay stuck, living our life in a semi-comatose state.

The key to realizing our vision is consistency, which contrasts with "when we can fit it in." Self-discipline is about exercising our commitment wholeheartedly on a daily basis. If we engage in discipline only half-heartedly or sporadically, we won't derive the benefit we require. It's therefore essential we are clear where we are going and what we want, and that we put in place the disciplines that can take us there.

I know in my life that if I'm not feeling a hundred percent, there's only one place I look for the cause: did I engage in my essential spiritual self-discipline that day? On those occasions I fail to do so, I take responsibility and choose differently the following day. A day without spiritual self-discipline isn't the same day as a day in which we are careful to discipline ourselves.

doing versus being

Most of us *do* self-discipline, which is quite different from *being* self-disciplined.

How can we tell the difference between *doing* self-discipline and *being* self-disciplined? There's a simple test. If we sense within ourselves any form of complaint about our self-discipline, we aren't in a state of *being*, which means self-discipline is still something we're *doing*.

When we're doing, we're disconnected from our own flow and hence have to force ourselves to perform. When we're being, we're in a *feeling* state that springs from the heart.

Part of people's struggle when they first implement self-discipline is an inability to be with what they feel. They try to force themselves to go contrary to the essence of their being. Consequently, their program of self-discipline doesn't survive long.

As an example of the difference between doing and being, I smile when people say, "I meditate." Those who are genuinely meditating don't need to tell anyone because it's not something they do, but a way of being in the world. Telling people we meditate is a sure sign we're doing instead of being.

Talking to others about our spiritual discipline feeds the ego. It's about making ourselves feel good. We want to look good in the spiritual arena. This usurps what it means to be spiritual.

There are obvious aspects of self-discipline we all should be participating in such as honoring the physical vessel in which our essence expresses itself. A day when we honor our body is a different day from a day in which we don't honor this vessel. Hence, keeping fit by exercising, eating healthily, getting enough sleep, and so on are a vital part of a conscious journey. To discipline ourselves in such ways is essential if we wish to engage life fully.

the live now philosophy

There is *only* the present moment: the future is an illusion, the past but an imagination. There is only the *now*, though we are hardly ever present in the now. When we live in the present moment, we gain the following benefits:

- We live at a higher level of awareness, experiencing no suffering.

- We enjoy oneness, not separateness, which causes us to always feel safe.

- We experience a sense of "arrival," with nowhere to get to.

The chart below examines the **Live Now Philosophy**:

WANT (Shape Shifting)	COMMITMENT (Transformation)
Humans having moments of spiritual enlightenment – disconnected from source	Spiritual beings managing their human egoic behaviour – connected to source
• Trying; Justification; Dissatisfaction	• Results
• Confusion – I don't know – *Grey Zone*	• Clarity – you do or don't – No Grey!
• DOING – Overwhelm; Struggle; Frustration; Anger; Anxiety	• BEING – In the Zone; Flow; Ease; Attract Synchronistic Opportunities
• More committed to the benefits of being disconnected	• Present to the costs of living life at a disconnected level
• Your version of integrity	• Operate at a high degree of integrity
• You operate over the top of everything	• You cannot be out, we clean everything up

STATE OF MIND	STATE OF MIND
Default (Edging God Out)	Power (Source)
Always Adding Meaning	No Meaning – Just What Is
Past & Future Projections	Living In The NOW Moment

Step 1   From moment to moment, we are either in our default state or in our power. In other words, we are either in the state of EGO (Edging God Out) or coming from our Source. We are always either adding meaning or accepting what is, feeding past or future-based projections or living in the moment. Ultimately, this is a choice based on awareness of what we are committed to.

Step 2 People say they want to change, but to be committed to change is a different ball game. We call it *shapeshifting* versus *transformation*. We are either human beings with moments of spiritual enlightenment, disconnected from source, or spiritual beings managing our human egoic behavior, connected to Source.

Step 3 We are either experiencing frustration through trying, justifying our failures, and reaping dissatisfaction, or we are producing results.

Step 4 We either hang out in confusion—living in the grey zone of "I don't know"—or we have great clarity, no grey, and are prepared to be responsible.

Step 5 We either operate from the state of *doing*, experiencing overwhelm, struggle, frustration, anger, and anxiety, or we operate from the state of *being*, experiencing the zone, ease, and flow, so that we become a conduit to attract synchronistic opportunities to ourselves.

Step 6 We are either committed to the "benefits" we experience in terms of getting to be right, making others wrong, feeling justified in our point of view, identifying ourselves as a victim, not having to be responsible, and getting to manipulate, dominate, and control, or we are present to the costs that rule our present and dictate our future.

Step 7 We either do "our version of integrity," or we live at a high level of integrity.

Step 8 We either operate over those areas of our life in which we haven't come to completion, or we clean everything up.

There are only ever two states for a human being to operate from: power or default. Which will you choose from this point on?

the power of gratitude

What I most want to share with you are a handful of self-discipline practices I've found helpful for placing myself on the path of presence each day.

One of my principal self-disciplines is my gratitude journal. As human beings, we continually want something other than what we have, so that we live in constant dissatisfaction. This is why, when a product comes on the market offering us something other than what we've already got, it takes on an air of mass hysteria. In contrast, someone who feels themselves to be in a state of abundance is grateful for every aspect of their life and doesn't need to get on the bandwagon of some motivational product before their world feels wonderful.

The entire marketing effort of the commercial world is aimed at people's insecurities and foibles. The amount of subliminal messaging used in the media is frightening. The danger is that the spiritual journey easily becomes subject to the lure of instant gratification, as we are offered secrets to attaining a world other than the one we are experiencing at this moment now.

The power of a gratitude journal is that it teaches us to be present to the magnificence of life. There are so many things on a daily basis for which we could be grateful, yet we aren't aware of most of them. Because we don't come from an abundance-based consciousness, wonderful things happen that simply fly under our radar.

I recommend to my clients that they write one page every day. Each day must be different from the day before. A day begun in gratitude is a different kind of day from a rushed day in which we don't savor what's happening in our life.

the low down on affirmations

Living consciously means envisioning what we know we are to do with our life as if it were already a reality. However, I'm not talking about envisioning in order to have an experience in a future-based timeframe.

The entire planet lives in a reality called "in order to." It's like being a good little boy or girl for God. We're really saying, "I'll do my gratitude journal in order to get something I want." Or we tell ourselves, "I'll affirm and visualize in order to manifest my goals." Or, "I'll sit in silence and meditate in order to feel better about myself."

The reality is that "in order to" one never feels satisfied.

What most mean when they speak of "affirming" and "visualizing" is really nothing more than wishful thinking. On the other hand, when I use the term "affirmation," I'm speaking about what author Michael Brown in his book *The Presence Process* calls a "presence activating statement." By a "presence activating statement," I mean a statement that comes from my inner *knowing*, which is fundamentally different from wishful thinking.

I like the term "presence activating statement" because it has a different feel from what people generally refer to as affirmations, which for many tend to be attempts to talk themselves into believing something. In my experience, most who use affirmations don't get the results they want and eventually give up. This is because they project their wishful thinking into some future-based moment.

What I'm referring to has nothing to do with *trying* to believe in something, but with manifesting what we are already invested in at a faith level. In other words, we're manifesting our *commitment* by making it the center of our *attention* and thereby activating everything we need to do in the present moment in order for it to come to fruition in its proper season.

We believe, not because we wish for something that sounds like a nice idea, but because of the call of our *inner knowing*. Our belief is the act of entrusting ourselves to what we are called to do in order to fulfill our legacy.

The clearer we are in our ability to visualize our life from inner knowing, the easier it is to manifest what we know. Daily visualizing of what we know in our essence can't fail to manifest because our vision flows from what *is*, not from wishful thinking. Hence, in my own life, as part of visualizing what's unfolding, I communicate daily with many people about things that are yet to happen. I communicate in such a way that we all know what will happen because I've already claimed it as a reality based on my inner knowing. If you were to ask anyone close to me about my vision, they would affirm this because they are my manifestation vehicles. I train people on how to communicate about me so that this level of resonance brings the vision into reality.

coming from a still center

The ability to simply be *with* ourselves is at the heart of conscious living. All of humanity's misery stems from our inability to be with ourselves in our ultimate aloneness.

Sitting in stillness in complete silence is a vital dimension of spiritual self-discipline. Until we are present, devoid of mental busyness, we can't comprehend, let alone appreciate, what it means to be connected to the Source of all *being*. Once we recognize we are all one with this Source, we can never be lonely. If we are to journey from unconsciousness to consciousness, our connectedness to everyone and everything must become our moment-by-moment experience. Entering into this experience has much to do with our ability to be with silence. A day without sitting in presence, prayer, contemplation, or meditation isn't of the same quality as a day approached from stillness.

To be alone with ourselves and express what we are feeling is freeing. In her book *The Artist's Way*, Julia Cameron teaches how to write in a free-flowing mode that helps us truly be with ourselves. Many of us like to write in our diary each day, which usually consists of recording what's happening in our life, but free-flowing writing is something different. What I love about the concept of "morning pages," as Julia terms them, is that we write with no prescribed format. We write what we're feeling, without constraint.

Stillness isn't the only dimension of being with ourselves. Often we're so preoccupied with fulfilling our duties and serving everybody else that we forget about ourselves. This is why I believe that, as part of our discipline, each of us needs a two-hour date with ourselves each week. On this date, we do only those things *we* want to do for our pleasure. We create space to be creative, or we take time to relax. Or, heaven help us, we pamper ourselves!

To be with ourselves requires us to respect ourselves. A vital discipline is to establish appropriate boundaries in our dealings with other people lest they trample all over us. Let me illustrate why this is important from the life of a tree. If we were to place a sapling that's no more than chest height in a paddock of cows, it wouldn't survive. But if we were to place a fence around it, water it, fertilize it, and prune it, the sapling would grow into a strong tree and we would then be able to remove the fence. In life, we need to educate people on how to treat us. There are times when we need to put boundaries in place on what's acceptable and unacceptable behavior.

For more than twenty years, I attracted mountains of verbal abuse. I couldn't work out why this was happening. I was a nice person who cared for people and went out of my way to support them, yet I was constantly dumped on from the greatest height, often viciously so. It went on until I realized that nobody can abuse us unless we allow it. In other words, I had unconsciously been allowing verbal abuse to be heaped on me all these years because such abuse validated my self-loathing.

The day I got that I no longer deserved to be abused on any level was the day the abuse stopped. I now partner people to become present to the cost of tolerating anything that doesn't serve them, giving them permission to claim their power in a way they've never experienced. Think about the number of people on the planet who at this very instant are hurting beyond comprehension as a result of all kinds of abuse. All these individuals need to do is arrive at the place where abuse is no longer acceptable to them.

It's from the strength of being a spiritually self-disciplined individual that we can commit ourselves to our legacy in complete trust, and allow ourselves to go into the glorious freefall of infinite consciousness.

PART II

my life
apprenticeship

In writing this second part of *Freefall*, I have chosen to speak out about what happened to me in my teens because I know that people who experience trauma at the hands of others to the degree I have are unable to reconcile the "what happened" if no one in society wants to hear it. Even though some of this section of the book may be difficult to hear, I ask that you hear these words.

When we are in the womb, it's the darkest yet the safest place to be. As we grow, we develop an aversion to what we perceive as darkness. In accessing the "dark night of my soul," I experienced the unexplainable. I went beyond the knowable. I emerged with an understanding that everything is in perfection and that what we perceive as dark is the access point for our enlightenment.

Everything I've learned has come to me from my life experience. So I want to share with you how I learned that our default identity must die, and how I entered into my true being, eventually becoming whole.

What this experience taught me, as I shared in Part I, is that allowing our default identity to die is drastically different from much of the self-improvement brought about by coaching and counseling. As a result of discovering the huge difference between self-improvement and the death of our default identity, I have even coached psychiatrists, working with individuals who are highly trained academically and accomplished specialists in their field, and been able to contribute to these professionals in a pioneering way.

I am interested in these professions leveraging off my knowledge because, since I have gone beyond the text books of old, there are experiences I have had that will enable them to facilitate transformational results in a way never before experienced. Having gone beyond the norm and come back of my own accord, I believe it's my responsibility to give back what I've learned.

Do you know what it is like to know you have the formula for alleviating people's pain both personally and professionally, yet few are listening to you? I believe I have the ability to change the way the human psyche works off the back of my personal traumatic experience. I am alive today to *give back what I have learned.*

In the chapters that follow, I offer my story and the lessons it imparts as a contribution to your development into a whole and fulfilled person whose life has meaning and purpose. *Freefall* is my legacy to humanity, so that others don't need to experience the kind of pain and despair I experienced.

Chapter 15

the day my life changed forever

Do you ever notice people's shoes? I do. Can you remember your first sexual experience? I'll tell you about mine. It's the reason I became so aware of shoes.

My first vacation job away from home was hiring out skis in National Park, Mount Ruapehu, New Zealand. I loved skiing. Any opportunity to be on the slopes was right up my alley, and now I was going to be paid to work in an activity that was my passion!

I was also excited about earning my own money for the first time and experiencing independence. My dad had encouraged my siblings and me to branch out on our own early, so here I was doing just that. I found it exhilarating.

It was August 1981, and I was sixteen. I arrived at the place where I was to board feeling not just fearless but gutsy. It was at a yummy ski lodge with a big open fireplace. I settled in and started work immediately. After ten days on the mountain, I received my first wage packet and thought I was the bee's knees.

By now I'd made friends with an eighteen-year-old female working at another hire place and we decided to hitchhike into the bright lights of the small town of Taumaranui. Hitchhiking was still a fairly standard means of transport in those days. I was so innocent, so naïvely unaware of the possibility of danger. Quite the opposite, I was excited to be venturing into the unknown for the first time.

At this point, I need to tell you how I was dressed on this particular day. You'll understand why I'm telling you this shortly. It was fairly cold, so I was wearing a heavy fair-isle Starsky and Hutch jersey knitted by my mother—a great big cardigan with a wide collar and huge pockets—together with black corduroy pants and ugg boots.

We arrived in Taumarunui, a town in the central North Island of New Zealand, and shopped as only girls can. I bought my own clothes for the first time and felt really pleased with myself. After we were done with the stores, my girlfriend suggested going for a drink at the local bar. I was underage, but didn't see the harm in it, so it didn't occur to me not to go with her. Perhaps there was also a bit of rebellion. In any case, it was important to me, as it is to most teens, to fit in and look cool.

We arrived at the bar around three o'clock in the afternoon, bought ourselves two jugs of beer, and proceeded to mingle with the locals, each of us gravitating toward different conversations. I was having a fun time chatting with people, happy just to be in a grownup scene. We didn't realize that from the moment we entered that public bar, we were being cased out by the Mongrel Mob, a New Zealand gang of mobsters.

At some point in the late afternoon, I became aware that my bag was missing. Instantly, I felt a sense of panic. It had in it my clothes, my money—everything. How would I get back to the ski lodge? I felt vulnerable and lost.

As I looked around for my girlfriend, I realized she was no longer in the bar. Feeling frightened, I went outside in search of her. Since it was winter in the southern hemisphere, it was dark already. It was also really cold now. I walked along the street, peering down an alleyway. I felt so alone.

The next moment, my life changed forever.

A vehicle screeched to a halt beside me and several males grabbed me and threw me inside. As the car sped off, I realized I was in the clutches of eight gang members.

This was my first taste of absolute terror.

Before I knew it, my clothes were torn off. Men sporting tattoos and hidden behind sunglasses, whose breath reeked of alcohol and whose body odor was nauseating, were groping me from every angle, manhandling me in a humiliating and violent manner. They were so strong and I felt so powerless, stripped not only of my clothes but also of my dignity. Swearing, cursing, pouring forth a torrent of verbal abuse—"Slut! Whore! Pakeha (Maori for white person) slag!"—they passed me back and forth across the seats, each of them abusing me. The terror of not knowing where we were going, nor knowing what was going to happen to me, was overwhelming. Throughout the ordeal, it was the not knowing that was the hardest to cope with.

The car finally stopped outside a house, where I was dragged out by my hair and pulled naked across the gravel kicking and screaming. The more I screamed, the more the men laughed. Now there were more voices and I could hear music. Inside the house, I was thrown onto a bed with a gang member. There was no eye contact. Though I did everything in my power to fight back, he pinned me down. As he tried to rape me, he passed out, lying comatose on top of me. My thoughts raced to how I might escape, but I was too terrified to move lest I wake him. Even though I could see a window and everything inside me screamed at me to get out, I was immobilized by my terror.

At that moment, five gang members burst into the room, grabbed me by my hair, and dragged me naked, kicking and screaming, past women and children sitting in the lounge room watching television. Out the back of the house, by the garage, gang members had gathered around a butchers block of wood. Cheering in anticipation, they began brawling over who would go first. Mob members were calling out to every male in earshot, "There's a woman on the block!"

Lying on my back, I stared dazed at a parade of gang members' faces as they raped me one after another after another, hour after hour. New Zealand's infamous Mongrel Mob had captured me and were penetrating me vaginally, anally, and orally, as well as ejaculating on me, urinating on me, beating me with their fists, and yelling obscenities at me. I screamed to the point I had no more voice.

As I was gagging from the constant thrusting into my throat, somebody was ejaculating on some other part of my body. My hair was a tangle, my skin wet and sticky with semen and urine and my own blood, my eyes bruised and swollen. The only emotion I could feel was anger that I seemed unable to lose consciousness.

They tossed me onto my front and started again. Lying face down, I could at last focus on something other than just my pain. I began noticing the shoes—so many shoes. Filthy, ragged shoes, with jeans or track pants bunched at the ankles. In fact, my most vivid memory of the ordeal is of watching constantly shifting shoes on the floor beneath where I lay on the block, every moment knowing that as long as there were shoes, more abuse was coming. They were the shoes of drunken men, foul with cigarette smoke and marijuana, cajoling each other, group pressure compelling even those who were reluctant to indulge themselves as a rite of initiation.

My thoughts raced: Where was Spirit? Why was this happening to me? What had I done to deserve such horror?

For me, on that block of wood, there were no answers and no escape. As the abuse continued, my soul split in two. It was the only thing it could do to release me from my torment. Everything hurt, but I didn't feel it now. From this point on, they could do anything they wanted to me: I had lost the fight. Though I was fully conscious, it was as if my consciousness had died. I just wished I could die.

It pissed them off that I wouldn't react anymore. They tried to goad me into reacting by yanking my hair and smashing bottles on the block where I lay. Broken glass was everywhere, and I was cut and bleeding inside and out.

The ordeal lasted for ten hours. I have no way of really knowing how many men raped me because the police were later only able to identify about seven, but for periods at a time there would be many men there all taking turns. It feels as if a hundred or more assaulted me.

I learned a lot about gang culture that night. One of my saddest realizations was that there were women around me, dancing while their men relieved themselves on me.

In the early hours of the morning, I was finally dragged off the block and thrown into the back of a sports utility. I dared to imagine it was all over. Instead of a reprieve, it began again. Three men were in the back of the ute with me and two in the front. The vehicle sped off. I reached a new level of terror: where was I being taken?

It was only much later that I learned I was being driven to Te Kuiti, one and a half hours away. While the vehicle careened down the road, the three in the back took turns at raping me in every orifice. After a while the car stopped so the driver and front passenger could swap places with two of the three in the back to take their turn also.

The vehicle came to a halt outside the mob hang-out in Te Kuiti. It was early morning, freezing cold, and I was left sprawled naked in the back of the ute, my first moments alone since the ordeal began. It felt as though some twenty minutes passed. Should I try to escape? I lay there wondering whether, if I were to knock on somebody's door naked and in such a beaten up condition, the residents would help me. And what if I tried to escape and the mob caught me? When I finally attempted to move, I was so cold, bruised, and in shock that I couldn't escape anyway. Still, I was hard on myself, asking myself: Why don't you escape, Sally?

Three gang members came to get me, again grabbing me by my hair and hauling me naked into the house. Tossed into a bedroom, I was raped repeatedly. During the ordeal, my prayer was finally answered and I lost consciousness.

The next thing I was aware of, a man opened the bedroom door and was surprised to find me there. I realized I had been alone in the house for hours. It turned out I was at the Te Kuiti home of the head of the mob and he hadn't expected to find me there. Tossing me some old track pants and a big jersey, he ordered, "Get dressed!" Then he demanded, "Where are you from?"

Somehow I managed to say, "National Park." He took me to his car, where a woman was sitting in the front seat. Without saying another word, he steered me into the back seat and closed the door. We drove in silence for an hour and a half. Not knowing where I was going, I was amazed to see us pull up outside where I was boarding.

The driver turned to me and said, "I want money."

"I don't have any."

"Go and find some!"

It was the middle of winter, dark, and I had been missing for forty-eight hours by this stage. I staggered towards the lights of the kitchen. Thinking back now, I can't imagine how I looked; but at the time, I was simply focused on getting money. When I opened the door, I found the full kitchen staff there. All I said was, "I need money."

"What happened to you?"

"I'll explain later." They must have heard the desperation in my voice, so without pressing me, they rallied around and came up with $40.

Back at the car, I handed over the money. Without a word, the mob king drove off. For what felt like a quarter of an hour, I stood in the middle of the road in the dark of night, freezing cold, the only light coming from the surrounding buildings. Nobody came outside to get me, and I was too terrified to move. I was quite simply dissociating, until the bitter cold winter air at last jolted me back into some semblance of rationality.

The only thing I could think of was that I had to have a bath.

Back in my lodgings, nobody was up. I went straight to the bathroom, drew a bath as deep as I could get it, and stayed there for hours, scrubbing and scrubbing until I was raw. Feeling no emotion, I didn't cry. I just sat in the water and scrubbed. Even after the water had gone cold, still I scrubbed. Would I ever rid myself of the stench?

I cannot explain how I felt in the twelve hours or so between coming back to reality and waking the following morning. Not only was I experiencing extreme loneliness, but I found myself analyzing myself over and over: Why me? What did I do to deserve this? How will I cope? It was a surreal experience in which I wasn't t in my body, but had died to myself as I knew myself. What was I to do? The fear I was experiencing was paralyzing, so I decided to sleep. It was simply impossible for me to "be with" what had happened to me. I wanted to erase every aspect of what had happened, yet I couldn't. Sleep, Sally, sleep.

The next morning, I could think only of not being late for work. I could hardly walk, so when I arrived, my supervisor took one look at me and, without a word, called the police. He was already concerned because I'd been missing for two whole days. Since I was underage, he felt a sense of responsibility for me. I could feel the care in his voice as he tried to talk to me, but I was in too deep a state of shock to answer. I desperately wanted to act as if nothing had happened. I especially didn't want anyone to phone my parents because it would be such a long journey for them to come get me.

Two police officers arrived, put me in their car, and took me to the local police station. Then came a barrage of questions: What happened? Why did you go into the public bar? Who were you with? Recount the entire event from beginning to end. I was so numb, yet the questioning continued relentlessly.

During the interview, I was asked to describe the vehicle. At that moment, a vehicle with a distinctive sound drove by the police station. "It sounded like that car outside," I said.

Now everything happened fast. I was put in a police car and we followed the Mongrel Mob utility to the mob hangout. Years later, I learned that this was how they apprehended two of the offenders who abducted me.

During the physical examination, I lay on a cold stainless steel table, again robbed of my dignity, again feeling like a piece of meat. All I wanted to do was die because once again I had no control over who was touching my body.

By the time the questioning was through, we had covered every moment of the time I had been missing. I just wanted to forget it all. The entire time, I showed no emotion. In fact, I didn't cry again until I was thirty years old because I believed crying showed weakness.

When my mother and father arrived, it was hard for them to know what to do. I didn't want anyone to touch me. My father had been a school guidance counselor. In his spare time, he also worked with youth and served in the community. He made a huge difference in the lives of many young people. Indeed, his whole life was about helping others. He had been brought up on Norman Vincent Peale, the godfather of the power of positive thinking, and he was such a positive man. I so admired his commitment and unfailing belief in what was possible. Yet now, faced with such an immense tragedy in the life of his own daughter, even he didn't know what to say. For those of you who are parents—those of you who have daughters—what the hell do you say to your daughter?

Though I was aware of my parents' concern, all I could feel was shame. We drove the six hours home to Gisborne mostly in silence.

I had survived, but my real ordeal was only about to begin.

Chapter 16

t w e n t y   y e a r s
i n   h i d i n g

One of the policemen who dealt with my case told me years later that mine was one of the worst reported gang rapes in New Zealand. I know of two others. One of the women involved committed suicide and the other ended up in a mental hospital.

During the year following my abduction and rape, I received absolutely no support psychologically. Post the event, I was expected to go back to school and act like nothing had happened. When I returned to school, I simply had to tell someone and found solace in sharing my experience with a friend. This was the first and last person I shared my experience with until I turned thirty years of age. To this day, that friend has no idea of the consolation she provided. She didn't judge me, but held my confidence and was there for me when I needed her. She remains today a soul-filled friend. I am alive because of her.

I internalized all my anger and as a result entered what became a life sentence of over twenty years of self-destruction and abuse. I was numb to feeling, dead to life, closed off to reality, barely functioning, unable to relate to anyone or anything. So consumed was I with my insane internal dialogue that I became increasingly isolated, so that no one could access me. Even if someone tried to access me, I wasn't *there*.

Becoming insular, I didn't want anyone to even come near me, let alone touch me. If anybody tried to get through to me, they had no chance of succeeding. Sports were the only remaining evidence that anything about me still "worked." It was the one area that gave me hope that not all of me had died.

I decided to leave school and move away from home. After a short course at secretarial college, I worked part time in a variety of jobs.

A year after the abduction, I met a handsome and gentle Maori man who treated me so well that he became the first male I allowed near me physically. He taught me that men could be safe. But I couldn't be present with how nice he was to me, so I ran from the relationship.

This began a cycle of repeat behavior that continued for more than twenty years. Whenever I met someone who appeared as though they would be good for me, something in me felt compelled to sabotage the relationship. A man would say he loved me, tell me I was beautiful, tell me I was great, but I couldn't hear it.

In August 1982, my case came to court. I vividly recall having to substantiate what had happened to me in so much heart-wrenching detail that I began to question who the perpetrator was and who the victim. I asked my mother not to attend because I couldn't stand the thought of her hearing what had happened. I wanted to safeguard her from truly knowing. My father couldn't be dissuaded. So, under oath, I had to relay blow by blow, in the presence of my father, what had been done to me.

To those conducting the trial, I had simply been gang raped. I felt they had no understanding of how much the whole experience had affected me. Twenty-three years later, when I was interviewed for a television program called *Police 10-7,* I learned that two of the five men who abducted me to Te Kuiti were sentenced to eight years in prison. At the time of the trial, I didn't realize this. I hadn't wanted to be there, so as soon as I had done what I needed to do, I got as far away as I could.

In my family, only my father knew in detail what actually happened to me. After the court case, he and I walked outside the court building. He offered me a cigarette, which was out of character for him. He must have known I had been filching his cigarettes since I was thirteen, but we had never discussed the fact I was a smoker. For me, this sharing of a cigarette was a defining moment in our relationship. It wasn't only my father's way of showing me how much he understood what I was going through, he was acknowledging me as an adult.

When something traumatic occurs, a lot of people focus on the incident itself, without realizing that it's the aftermath that takes the greatest toll on the victim. This is why I say that, when I emerged alive from the abduction and rape, my ordeal was only just beginning.

trying to feel "okay"

I decided to move to Franz Josef in New Zealand's South Island. Though I was still young, I wasn't afraid of moving so far from home. On the contrary, the resilience generated by surviving the abduction put me in good stead for stepping out.

Franz Josef is a truly beautiful part of New Zealand, so it was a great experience to live and work there. Nobody knew my past, which meant I could present whatever persona I wished. Like many of the Tourist Hotel Corporation hotels in New Zealand, the Franz Josef was situated in a remote resort location, so the only social environment in which we could congregate was the public bar. This became my home away from home, even though I was still underage.

By this time, I would do anything to drown the pain of what had happened to me. Consequently, I worked hard but partied even harder. Rum and coke, and gin and tonic, were pretty much my standard drinks. Not to mention that I was a huge shot tippler! I was proud no one could drink me under the table. What a thing to be proud of, but I was! In those days, I latched onto anything that validated my worth. Drinking and drugs were my solace, which meant that sometimes I lost days on binges. As a result, my weight was creeping up too, despite smoking sixty cigarettes a day.

Having felt different all my life, I wanted to be told I was okay, and I wanted to belong. I became proficient at pool, so much so that people used to come into the bar just to watch me play. Apart from sports, this was my first experience of being good at anything.

The bar was a way for me to belong. Yet I wanted more than to just belong: I wanted someone to love me.

Darren was a carpenter who whistled at me whenever I walked past a building site in the Franz Josef village. I fell for him. Because his sister had been raped by his father, I felt a kindred spirit and opened up, for the first time talking about what had happened to me. He was also the first man with whom I experienced sexual intimacy after my ordeal, and he proved to be a godsend. When I found out he was already engaged to be married, I was devastated. When I let him go, he gave me a Maori carving, which he explained represented "love split between two people." I became friends with his fiancée. As my way of getting back at him, I also slept with his best friend, which hurt him. I regret a lot of things about the way I lived my life, but at the time I knew no different. I was barely hanging on.

During my time at Franz Josef, my brother Mark died. This devastated me, for I was the last one to spend time with him. He had visited me at Franz Josef and we had the best time. I was so proud to hang with my bro. He returned to the North Island after his visit and ended up in a car accident on Boxing Day, 1983. I loved him, and even now know he is with me. I too almost died in a car accident in which I was thrown head first through the windshield and knocked unconscious. I had wanted to die, but I thrived on the attention I received when I found myself still alive following the accident.

I craved attention so much now that I longed for a child and made up a story that I had been pregnant with Darren's. How disastrous having a child would have been, given my condition! I was in no fit state to look after myself, let alone a child.

Still, I needed to fantasize that there was someone in the world who loved me unconditionally. So for the next eleven years, whenever I met anybody new, I told them I had given birth to a love child, for which I had false photos, a name, and names for the adopting parents.

Remembering how my soul split into two when I was lying on that block back in my darkest hours, I now have compassion for the way I portrayed myself to the world as a quite different person from who I really was. Years later, after a course that taught me the power of integrity, I cleaned up with every single person with whom I had shared my fabrication. It was doubly hard to tell the truth because few knew anything about the gang rape that had given rise to the lie. When I told people what had happened to me, most reacted with disbelief. Getting honest didn't come easily.

the sun shines through for a moment

When I caught the assistant manager of the hotel stealing money out of the till and reported it to the general manager, I didn't realize the two were close friends. I was asked to resign. I couldn't believe this was happening to me and felt a tremendous sense of betrayal coupled with shame. However, something in me was determined not to be wronged in this way, so I took the Tourist Hotel Corporation to court.

In return for discontinuing the case, I was promised I could stay in the chain's employ. But this meant I was relegated to the position of housemaid, which in those days was the lowest of the low. I felt utterly demoralized, a feeling that was compounded by being ostracized by my peers for bringing disgrace to the hotel. I could have left to save face, but something in me compelled me to stay and keep my dignity. Instead of quitting, I was determined to be the best housemaid I could be. In fact, I enjoyed being a housemaid even though it was backbreaking work because the housekeeping crew made me feel part of the team and were kind to me.

While I was polishing the brass edge of the steps at the entrance to the hotel one day, a duty manager stepped on the newly polished surface, smeared it with his foot, looked at me degradingly, and walked off. I owe this man gratitude, because in that moment I thought, "How dare you!" I knew I deserved better than this and chose to leave Franz Josef. The episode turned out to be a fledgling step in the *real* me "showing up" in my life.

By now I was well on my way along a journey of sexual addiction that was to last until I was thirty-seven. On the one hand, it didn't matter what men did to my body because it felt separate from me. I actually believed my body deserved to be abused because I saw it as worthless. On the other hand, I badly needed some form of external validation of my worth and became the "girl about town" in every sense of the expression. There was nothing I wouldn't do in search of the validation I craved.

A Samoan man fell for me. A respected *maitre d'* in the hotel business, he was professional, good looking, fit, healthy, and made me laugh. My relationship with Sam was my first and last real relationship. We were together off and on for two years, the longest I'd ever stayed with a man. In 1984, we transferred together to the Tourist Hotel Corporation Chateau in the North Island, where we lived for eighteen months. The Chateau is at Mount Ruapehu, only an hour from Taumarunui where my ordeal began. My time at the Chateau was healing for me and I have many fond memories of that period. I made friends who are still in my life, excelled in my work, gained confidence in my ability, and was happy.

Then came the day I found Sam in bed with a man. That it was a man, not a woman, brought my feelings about myself to a head. This was in a small town, where Sam held a position of authority within the hotel. Because everybody knew what had happened, I felt humiliated all over again.

From that moment, I became obsessed with sexuality. Countless one-night stands followed with bus drivers, house guests, locals, any male. The sex didn't mean anything to me. I yearned to be wanted and needed. Sleeping with a guy put another notch in my belt, which felt like getting my own back on the world.

So there I was, living and working at a ski field but not skiing much because I was too busy drinking and recovering from hangovers. I almost lived at the Whakapapa Tavern and may as well have had the hotel deposit my wages there.

With two different personae, I operated right over the top of my pain.

"why does this keep happening to me?"

In my double life, I developed a bond with a woman named Rebecca, and with her I began the long journey to being able to trust again.

We decided to go to London together, working for Tom Eden and Associates, The Tourist Hotel Corporation's representatives in London, charged with selling New Zealand as a destination to the British. In London, people I was close to knew nothing of the life I really led. I was at the height of my sexual addiction. If I didn't score, I felt I wasn't good enough. It was the numbers that fed my sense of validity. Nothing was outside the limits of what I'd try.

Travel became a way of escaping the memory of my past. I visited France, skiing at Val d'Isere, as well as Bavaria and Switzerland. For my twenty-first birthday, I celebrated in Santorini, Greece.

For me, America had always represented freedom, so I flew with a female friend to Lake Tahoe intending to ski and then continue on to New Zealand. Though we had the correct documents for entering the United States, we hadn't yet purchased our ongoing tickets. As a consequence, we were suspected of trying to enter the country to work illegally, which led to incarceration in Anaheim, California. During the three days we were in Anaheim prison, I wasn't allowed to see my friend and was denied even a single phone call. As with the abduction at Taumarunui, I was again being held against my will, once more experiencing myself as all alone and terrified.

Because many Mexicans who cross the border were thrown into jail for three months, we were advised not to contest the case. So entirely out of fear, I appeared in court and admitted I was guilty of a crime I had never committed. We each paid a fine of $500 and endured the humiliation of being handcuffed, escorted onto an aircraft bound for London, and only then given our passports. How, I asked myself, could I be humiliated again like this? What was it about me that seemed to *attract* humiliation?

I feel such a sadness for who I was at twenty-one. Though I was outwardly strong and confident, I was frightened inside and for the first time in a long while felt utterly vulnerable. Now more than ever, I trusted nobody and let no one into my inner world. I was struggling to stay alive within my *own* prison walls.

feeling like a freak

After London, I went to work in a hotel at Ayers Rock in the heart of Australia. Though I had many good experiences, all the time I was dying inside, so that the thought of suicide came to me more and more. The only thing that kept me from ending my life—and I do mean the only thing—was that, after my brother's death, I just couldn't bring more shame and pain to my family.

It was at Ayers Rock that I had my first taste of feeling like a freak. Although I learned early in my life that it wasn't safe to be a woman, I was astonished at how often, regardless of whether I dressed in business attire or evening dress, people questioned whether I even was a woman.

I experienced a tremendous need to validate that I was a woman by going to bed with men, yet I increasingly felt I was a freak. Consequently, I sabotaged many a relationship with men who had the potential to truly care for me. I believed that if they were to spend any length of time with me, their friends would accuse them of dating a man dressed as a woman. I would have welcomed the usual issues most couples have to deal with! They paled compared to the embarrassment of watching a man who was interested in me struggle with his own identity.

Unbeknown to me, I was operating from masculine energy more than feminine energy because I felt unsafe being a woman. How I came across was actually nothing more than a projection of my own fear.

Do you know how many times in the course of the day I have to deal with the effect my voice has on people? Each time is a vivid reminder of what was done to my vocal chords. It takes more than wearing a dress to exude femininity when your natural female voice has been destroyed and your voice is deep, almost like a man's. When someone calls and asks for Sally Anderson, I have to explain to them that I *am* Sally and not Mr. Anderson. Ninety-nine percent of the phone calls I make, whether to ask for a number from information, place an order for pizza, or at a drive-through ordering a takeaway, I'm addressed as Mr. Anderson.

If I stopped to think about this and had to try to be "positive" about it, I wouldn't get out of bed in the morning. But that's the point: I don't think about it these days. I don't entertain it at all. It took me twenty years to no longer allow the daily reality of my voice to impact me, but I finally realized that my past can have no effect on my present state of mind unless I allow it. When a voice on the other end of the line says, "How are you today Mr. Anderson?" I don't even bother correcting them. To this day, when speaker bureaus question the depth of my voice, they tend to change their tune when I explain, "I have screamed beyond all comprehension of screaming, and received untold oral abuse, to the point that my vocal cords were damaged."

how we form our default identity

Do you know what it's like to live a life in which you have no freedom to be yourself because you are too ashamed of what you represent?

You may well, because countless people feel this way about themselves. Why? Often for no reason other than that, when we were young, someone told us we were ugly, dumb, or fat. Even though what they told us may have had no validity, we adopted their projection and operated from this identity. Unless something wakes us up to who we really are, we then live out of this paradigm for the rest of our life.

Take a client of mine called Susan who shared with me that when she was eleven, her father commented quite flippantly one day, "You're fat." This little girl then chose to adopt this belief about herself. Today, at the age of sixty-five, she's still living from this belief, which has denied her the ability to celebrate her body. Her entire life, she has felt inhibited intimately and sexually, unable to enjoy a full expression of her physicality, all because of a statement somebody made when she was nine! The irony is there's no truth to what she believes about herself.

In all of our lives, there are defining periods that create the default identity from which we then live. In fact, it's been shown there are three distinct periods in our life during which we form our self-definition. They occur between the ages of three and five, five and twelve, and twelve and twenty-one.

In my own case, the first defining moment I remember came on my first day at school. I had red hair—the only redhead in our family—with freckles, pale skin, and a Canadian accent. The accent came from having lived in Canada for three and a half years beginning when I was two because of my dad's career. That I didn't look the same, sound the same, or think the same as the majority of the children at my New Zealand school defined me as "different." So many of my earliest memories are about being different and it was never a positive feeling. Imagine: I am six, and my self-identity is that I'm different! All I wanted was to be like everybody else so I would fit in.

My second defining moment occurred at the age of twelve when a science teacher asked us to write our names. I always printed, always. I found printing a lot clearer and never felt the need to write. Because I printed my name rather than writing it, I was told in front of the entire class that I was "stupid." I already felt bad enough because I was a year behind my own age group since we didn't return from Canada until I was six, which meant I didn't start school when New

Zealanders start school. For the next twenty years, I believed I was dumb and hence performed miserably academically.

To reinforce this view of myself, I associated with people who were academically high achievers. This enabled me to "prove" to myself how dumb I was and hence validated the belief I adopted in science class that day. Soon I was finding evidence everywhere of how dumb I was as I tried to compete but was already convinced I couldn't match up. At age fifteen, I failed the examination for the school certificate, which everyone has to pass in New Zealand. So I had to go back to school for another year and re-sit the exam, the sheer embarrassment of which validated my belief that I really was dumb!

A third defining moment followed when, at the age of sixteen, the abduction and gang rape occurred, which caused me to feel utterly unlovable for more than two decades. I was revolted at the mere sight of myself, to the extent that peering at myself in a mirror felt like looking at a seething mass of maggots. It's amazing how a person can function at all in life when they experience this degree of self-loathing!

From the age of sixteen until I was thirty-five, I never allowed myself to look at my face without makeup, and no one else ever saw me without makeup. I wore a perpetual mask because I believed that if anyone saw behind the mask, they wouldn't be able to handle such a revolting sight. A face with makeup was the only way I could face the world!

When we wear such a mask 24/7, which in my case meant I was never able to swim for fear the mask might wash off, there's no freedom. Going on vacation with friends, I restricted myself to those activities in which I could wear full-on makeup. I never allowed a man to kiss me in public because it might remove some of my makeup. If I slept with a man, he was only allowed to kiss me in the dark. Before he awakened in the morning, I plastered on a full face and climbed back into bed so he never saw me without makeup. The thought of being seen without makeup was annihilating. Imagine the effort this required.

What was true of my face was also true of my body. I never went out in the sun because I believed my body was too abhorrent to be seen uncovered. So while most people enjoyed summer, I dreaded it. Winter was my favorite time of year because it was when I could most cover my body. Once, I even went through three winters in a row by traveling to avoid summer, claiming it was because I loved skiing. The truth was I couldn't bear being in my body and didn't want it seen.

But as I'm about to share with you, beneath all of my woundedness lay my real self—a person who had never been hurt in my entire life. Only my default identity had been wounded, and ultimately it has no substance.

I was ready to begin the journey home to myself.

Chapter 17

the return home

Intuitively, I must have known that being overseas allowed me a period of escape in which I didn't have to face up to my demons. Deciding to come home was a signal to me that there was a better way than running from myself. Consequently, part of me was excited about returning to New Zealand and part of me was in trepidation at facing what my homeland represented for me.

It was 1987, and the girl who returned to Auckland wasn't the same one who had left two years earlier. I was twenty-one going on twenty-two. Although I'd always had an interest in self-development and read many books exploring the human psyche, it wasn't until now I was at last prepared to explore *myself*.

I realized I needed something that would give me a sense of why I was the way I was, why I thought the way I thought, and why I behaved the way I behaved. So I started taking self-help courses with a vengeance. Given that I was an addict in many other ways, it was natural for me to become a course junkie, addicted to understanding and making sense of what had happened to me.

If we imagine we can operate over the top of what we know intuitively, we then have to live with our conscience. I talk about conscience as first a tap on the shoulder, then a four-by-two at the back of the head, and finally a Mack truck. I've always tended to learn my most life-changing lessons only at the Mack truck stage. Why does it take a dramatic experience before we get down on our knees with nowhere else to go but within ourselves?

Looking back now, I'm saddened that I didn't realize the answers to life actually lay within me. All I ever did was look outside myself for solutions, whether in a book, a course, or a guru. I believed everybody had the right advice for me except *myself.* I had spent my life looking outside of myself for answers but it hadn't worked. Now there really was nowhere else for me to go but within.

It's sad that it usually takes a hugely painful wake up call to get our attention, and I realize now there's another way. But I only know this because I lived at the extremity of dysfunctional behavior. It isn't until we reach the point where we enter a dark night of the soul that we realize we have been feeling a tap on the shoulder for a long time but have chosen not to listen.

Finally, we have no choice but to listen.

love wooing us back

To most of us, the idea of the dark night of the soul seems frightening. Yet every aspect of this experience, no matter how scary it may feel, is actually nothing but love wooing us back to our true self.

For me, the dark night of the soul meant learning there was nowhere else to go but to surrender to something far greater than myself. For the first time in my life, I knew what it meant to trust my faith.

Most people's relationship with faith is intellectual. Having been a control freak all my life, I learned through many dark-night-of-the-soul experiences that faith can't be acquired through the intellect. In fact, faith isn't something we acquire at all. It's something we already have that we exercise through surrendering to the unknown—which, ironically, is the thing we are afraid of the most.

As this life-changing awareness dawned, I applied for a transfer to the Sheraton, Auckland, and was accepted as a receptionist on the front desk. I had only ever worked in a resort environment, where the way of interacting was different from that of the fast-paced corporate world. In my new corporate environment, there was no time for personal interaction. What a contrast to my experience at Ayers Rock! Something was missing for me in this big city setting. I found it almost soulless after my time at The Rock. I missed the people component a resort provided.

Working in the corporate environment was about processing numbers. I felt I had become a number in the system and recoiled inside myself. This inaugurated a period of feeling really separate from society. Though I made friends, had a lot of laughs, and learned a lot at Sheraton Auckland, after six months I knew it wasn't for me.

The general manager of the Chateau had been my first mentor and I knew one of his dreams had always been to become general manager in Queenstown in the South Island of New Zealand. When I learned he was now in his dream job, I wrote and asked if I could work for him again. To my delight, he invited me to join the team for the launch of a new hotel that coming winter. By the time I was 23, I was in my element. I worked my way up through the ranks and eventually became front office manager of the newest hotel in Queenstown.

As I look back, I shudder at my management of staff because I placed unrealistically high standards on myself and then transferred these onto everyone else. Although I was fair with staff, I showed little compassion. How could I? I had no compassion for myself.

the challenge of being both seen and heard

Every night was a Friday night for me and I lived it to the max. On a regular basis, I would consume a cask of port, followed by two to three bottles of wine, then switch to shots in the early hours of the morning. There was little reprieve from my addictive personality. My ethos was work hard, play hard, party hard. I have no idea how my body coped with the abuse I put it through. Amazingly, I was an exemplary employee the entire two years I was there.

An opportunity for advancement came when I was noticed by the Deputy Chief Executive of the Tourist Hotel Corporation. I knew nothing about him. However, he had heard of me and handpicked me for a position on the systems team based in Wellington. Within three months I had graduated to the position of reservations manager. I was only twenty-three years old and this was one of the most senior positions in the Tourist Hotel Corporation. It was the start of my senior corporate career.

I'm still astonished at the angels the universe sent to me in the guise of mentors who often saw possibilities in me well before I did. My mentor at that time will never know the lifeline he handed me. Through mounting external evidence, I was becoming aware I mattered. This began at last to generate within me a belief in myself.

As I embarked on a journey of career development, there were countless times when I doubted my ability, but you would never have known. I never, ever let it show. I presented to the world a person who was always together, make-up immaculate, clothing exemplary. To the outside world, I was invincible. If only they knew the truth! For throughout that time, there wasn't a day when I didn't have to deal with the thought of suicide.

I'm in no way condoning suicide, but after two decades of experiencing a suicidal conversation in my head, I believe I understand the nuances of suicide from every angle. People who commit suicide aren't taking the easy option. Until you walk in their shoes, you can't comprehend the inner world that leads up to the act itself. Having lived in the dark side of my personality for two decades, I understood in ways others simply can't understand. I believe there are many ways one can mask suicide, and I believe the documented symptoms aren't the only symptoms that are synonymous with feeling suicidal. It's for these reasons that I want to teach people there's another way.

As I moved deeper into the corporate world, I was required to speak in public. I was so fearful of getting up in front of an audience that I would be physically sick. I just died inside each and every time. Finally, it came time to face my fear, which proved to be a challenging experience.

To obtain expert help, I joined Toastmasters. The regular meetings taught me the nuances of professional speaking, but the most important aspect was developing confidence in myself. Toastmasters has a feature called table topics in which you are asked to stand and speak for one minute on a topic given to you seconds before you stand up. The aim is to teach you to speak off the cuff so you never get caught out. I used to hate table topics! Just standing up and being seen by a roomful of people was a terrifying ordeal, let alone saying anything. It took me many months to overcome the immobilizing fear of being seen.

Whenever I spoke in public, I did everything I could to act the part of a seasoned speaker. I was adept at cultivating a façade and could easily adopt a fictitious persona. For a time I was a complete fraud. I could stand up and speak as an actor, but heaven forbid that I should allow an audience to really *see* me.

My breakthrough came unexpectedly. When a member of the executive team was given a keynote speaking opportunity, it was standard procedure to make the presentation to their colleagues beforehand. When it was my turn, I would prepare 1000%. I did hours and hours of work to ensure that, heaven help me, I didn't appear dumb.

One particular day, I felt well prepared and confident my delivery would impress. So it was a shock when, after I had been speaking for only a short time, the managing director of the company interrupted. "What are you doing?" he demanded.

I was devastated. "What do you mean? I'm doing what I thought you wanted me to do."

He responded: "Sally, but where are *you?*"

My mind raced. What was he saying? Did he mean he wanted *me* up there in front of the entire executive team? *Me?* Why would he want *me?* I had only ever given a presentation on the basis of what I thought people wanted to hear, not from what I myself thought.

I responded: "Do you mean you wish me to do this presentation the way I would really want to do it?"

He said: "Sally, do you think I pay you the money I do to have anything but *you?*"

In professional speaking circles, they say you've arrived as a speaker when you are paid a huge amount of money to be *yourself.* I left the office and rewrote the presentation. From that day forward, I never again presented with notes. The managing director had given me the greatest gift a person can give another, the gift of feeling free to be myself. He had handed me a get-out-of-jail-free card and I flew!

Do I experience immense fear each and every time I speak now? Without a doubt. It's human to experience fear. But these days I don't make it mean anything. The first phase of transcending fear is the ability to become an observer of our fear rather than being immersed in it. When we are able to allow fear to simply be, without resisting it, it dissipates. I also learned that public speaking is about *intimacy:* "into me see." It was my journey home to truly being seen!

the value of judgment

Public speaking generated an enormous amount of fear in me since it placed me in the spotlight more intensely than any other aspect of my life. Suddenly, all eyes were on me and it was hard not to feel as though I was being critiqued, assessed, and judged.

What I've learned is to have compassion for myself in my fear. If I'm fearful before an audience because I imagine they might judge me, I say bring it on because I now believe the judgment meted out to us not only by ourselves but also by others is our chance to develop mastery of the art of compassion.

The more you judge me, the more you teach me to have compassion for the shoes you walk in. If your judgment of me is extreme, it speaks volumes for how painful your world must be. The more you project onto me that I'm the devil incarnate, the more I learn to be like a leaf on a river. If we are to believe in Jesus, he and his disciples were bitterly misjudged and persecuted, though they were masters at showing compassion.

When I learned to surrender to compassion, I made a request of Spirit to send into my life as many people as possible to assess and judge me because therein lay my ability to understand what it really means to have compassion. The worse someone's behavior was, the greater the opportunity it afforded for me to love them.

This challenge came to a head when the New Zealand television program *60 Minutes* chose to interview me on Sunday, September 13, 2004. It rated as the highest watched *60 Minutes* segment ever in the history of the program in New Zealand. The documentary won the best Human Relations Award at the Qantas Media Awards in 2005.

I decided to do the documentary because I wanted to be an inspiration to people, showing them they can turn their lives around in a positive direction. I wanted them to know we have a choice: we can live a destructive life because we allow our past to rule us, or we can use our past as a vehicle of transformation.

It was also important for me to find my voice on my own trauma before the mass public, thereby giving a voice to those who have never had a voice. The healing process can only occur when people are no longer ashamed of what has occurred in their past. And, too, this was a way for me to gain completion on what had been twenty years of silence.

During the interview, I spoke face-to-face with the past president of the Taumaranui chapter of the Mongrel Mob. Though he couldn't recall whether he was present at the time of my abduction and was one of the men who raped me, the police suspect he was in fact one of my attackers. He agreed to appear on the show with me because his own life had changed dramatically. Free of the gang for fifteen years, he now counsels inmates recently released from jail. Admitting he had raped many women with the Mongrel Mob, he wanted to talk because he felt it could help other victims. He was able to ask for forgiveness.

Chapter 18

c l i m b i n g   m y   e v e r e s t

It seems that everyone has an Everest, a seemingly insurmountable obstacle. What would your life look like if you climbed your Everest?

You might think my Everest was being able to forgive my abductors. People say to me, often quite angrily, "How can you forgive the Mongrel Mob for what they did?"

This was not my Everest. In fact, I say to those who ask me how I can forgive, "You seem to be more angry than I am, yet I was the one who went through the experience!" I can take this approach because I long ago came to the realization that *the only person who loses out from an inability to forgive is the person who can't forgive.*

Most people's relationship to forgiveness revolves around the offending party. We are going to find it difficult to forgive when our focus is primarily on the individual or individuals who perpetrated the act. Once we realize that forgiveness is perhaps ten percent about the other party and ninety percent about what we do to ourselves as a result of what was done to us, we no longer struggle with forgiving someone. I endured a forty-eight-hour nightmare, but I was the one who then sentenced myself to twenty-plus years.

I did it to *myself.* Nobody did it to me.

Someone says, "You hurt me!" Nobody can hurt us unless we allow it. And if we allow it, we're getting something out of it. Anything done to us can only have power over us if we feed it.

For example, if we were victims of incest when we were in our teens and we're now sixty-five years of age, we've experienced half a century of pain because we fed ourselves a host of self-talk about what was done to us.

When we don't feed what happened to us, it remains a horrible episode in our life but it doesn't in any way define us and thereby ruin our life. The pain was *then,* as long as the experience lasted. There's no reason for this pain to be in our life *now.* When we live in the now, nothing can be in our life unless we're the one putting it there.

When a traumatic incident occurs, we experience shame. As a result, we tend not to speak out about our experience. To heal, one needs to speak out about what happened. If we're still triggered by our past, then we're *not* healed. Healing means our past doesn't "have" us at any level. Only when this is the case are we equipped to help others heal.

The past is but a thought. It lives nowhere other than in our thoughts. So why do we keep feeding such thoughts when they don't serve us? We feed them because they keep our default identity in place, which is a victim status in which we feel powerless to change our situation.

As for the future, it too is nothing but a projection of what we're thinking in the now. When we're living in our thoughts instead of in reality, how can we possibly hope to be content?

reaching for success

By 1992, the Tourist Hotel Corporation had merged with Southern Pacific Hotel Corporation, the largest hotel chain in the South Pacific at the time. At the age of twenty-seven, I was in the role of reservations sales and systems manager, accountable for ninety hotels throughout the region. Our head office was based in Sydney, so for twelve months I travelled there weekly. Because I excelled in my position, I was chosen to be part of an international team to travel frequently to the United States, Europe, and the United Kingdom, investigating automation within central reservation systems.

To the outside world, I was a senior corporate executive. Inside myself, I was slowly dying. At no point did my sexual addiction stop. I still lived according to my work hard, play hard, party hard philosophy. All this time later, I'm amazed how, given that I had unprotected sex with hundreds of men, I never contracted AIDS, a sexually transmitted disease, or fell pregnant.

Years later, a book called *I Have Life* had a profound impact on me. A girlfriend asked me why I wasn't angry about what had happened to me. In fact, she was angry that I wasn't angry, so she gave me this book to read. It was the autobiography of a woman who had been abducted and raped by two men in South Africa. I was moved by a part of the book that spoke of *rape and abduction syndrome*. Back in 1981, there was little support for those who had been raped or abducted. As a result of reading this book, I realized the reason I wasn't angry was that, because I had received no counseling of any description, I was too busy just surviving to be aware of the impact of what had happened to me. As I read, I felt as though I'd been suffering from a disease without even knowing such a disease existed. Now I was finally finding out that the syndrome I was experiencing had a name and recognized side effects. Sufferers can go one of two ways: they either lock their doors and are paranoid about their safety, or they have total disregard for their safety and constantly put themselves at risk. In the early days after my abduction and rape, I chose isolation; later I chose to keep putting myself in risky situations. In neither of these reactions was I being who I truly am.

As I pursued my dangerous course, I became strategic in the way I sought out men, which is ironic given what, twenty-seven years later, I learned about my abduction. As mentioned earlier, from the minute I set foot in that bar I was being cased out by the Mongrel Mob. The role of the local who chatted me up was to pick the Mob's fresh piece of meat for the day. So now, I would go to a public bar, choose the best-looking man in the room, and play a game with myself to see whether I could pull him. At times, I would even grade myself on my ability to attract a man into my web. At no point throughout those years of sexual addiction did I ever allow a man to make love to me. Instead, I became a professional performer who would take men into realms of extremity beyond their wildest dreams.

queen of victim

My next career shift was to Melbourne, Australia. I did a lot of personal development work in Melbourne. For one thing, I joined Landmark Education and I credit this education with keeping me alive at the time.

In a course at the age of thirty, in front of three hundred people, the leader called me the Queen of Victim. I didn't like that. My perception of a victim was one of weakness and I didn't see myself as weak. Then he explained he used the word "victim" in terms of being powerless to change a specific situation, not powerless in general. This resonated with me and led me into an intense immersion in every program they offered. For five years I journeyed in the Landmark curriculum.

During this time, I talked for the first time about my abduction, breaking new ground by accessing my emotions and crying. I came to see that to experience emotion isn't a weakness but a strength. To reveal one's past isn't something to be ashamed of but to be honored. The sense of liberation after years of suppression was life-altering.

A significant event occurred that became a pivotal moment for me. In a group discussion, we were asked to talk with a fellow participant about something we had always wanted to ask but never had. The man I paired off with seemed uncomfortable about asking his question so I said, "There's nothing you can say I haven't heard before, so lay it on me."

He replied, "Sally, I don't know how to ask this, really I don't."

I reiterated that whatever he asked would be fine. In the next breath, he said, "Ever since you started this program, I've been trying to work out whether you're a man or a woman. Are you one of those transvestites?"

To hide my devastation, I responded: "Hey, thanks for sharing! I really appreciate your honesty. Just for the record, I'm a woman. But I realize what it must have taken for you to broach this with me." Though on the inside I found myself recoiling, I placated the situation. It wasn't so much his question that troubled me, since I'd been asked this so many times. It was that he seemed revolted just by my presence.

Back in the group, as everyone shared their experience of the exercise, I spiraled down into myself, devastated. When the course leader asked about my experience, I didn't wish to respond. However, he stayed with me until I reported what had happened. Then I challenged: "Bet that's one for the books!" I just had to be dramatic. Upon which I burst into tears and ran from the room.

Three guys chased after me. While two of them tried to placate the situation, the third called me to account: "Sally Anderson, you know who you are. You know you are a powerful, beautiful woman. How dare you take this on as if it's the truth! Get back into that room and take your power back." It was the way he said it. Like a lightning bolt, his words hit me and I instantly acted upon them. To this day, this man is a wonderful friend.

Years later I realized how powerful I used to be in my victim behavior, using classroom dramatics to draw attention to myself. Don't get me wrong: I'm not condoning what happened or lessening the impact of years of people's projection. All I know is that it wasn't safe to be a woman. I now have compassion for the many years in which I endured feeling like a freak to the world.

I experienced further compassion for myself when I was faced with two big fears in life: public speaking, which involved being truly seen; and the Mongrel Mob, who would put a hit out on me if I went public about my past. This was a real fear for me! Looking back, I have huge compassion for myself for embracing this fear and taking my power back, enabling me to own my power in a way I had never experienced.

learning to play the game of life

Returning to New Zealand at the age of thirty-three, I experienced one disappointment after another in terms of employment. Friends went away. I got into debt. This caused me to lose my confidence. I retreated into what I then thought of as *depression*, in which I once again revisited my suicidal tendencies.

When some friends offered me a housesitting job for two weeks, I accepted. In that two-week period, I chose to dig deep inside myself asking: If I were to go out on my own in business, what am I truly passionate about? What would my company be called? What would it look like? I didn't even consider entertaining the "how." I simply enquired of myself: What am I doing here on Earth?

Although this two-week period was one of my darkest times, it saw me emerge to reclaim my power. I came up with the company name Stepping Out, borrowed $500 from a friend, had business cards printed, and sent a flyer out to twenty consultancy companies. By this time I had been unemployed for eight months, my confidence was at its lowest ebb, and I was completely strapped financially. Within twenty-four hours, I was called in to discuss a position with a company that at the time was one of the most high-profile project management companies in New Zealand.

After three intense interviews, they asked me what I wanted to earn. At this point I would have accepted anything. Don't ask me why, but I decided to play a game. Although part of me would have been happy to accept a salary of $30,000, I immediately thought of how I'd always wanted to earn a six-figure salary. So I asked for $100,000 and shook in my boots thinking they would laugh at me. The next day, they presented me with a contract, having accepted my request. I learned that if you believe in yourself, life is in fact a game.

Over the next four years, I led major cultural change initiatives in three separate organizations and found myself working at board level. Did I experience fear each and every time I took on a challenge? Indeed. For instance, there was the time I assumed the role of program director for a high-profile New Zealand company and within days also took on the role of chief information officer. At moments during that assignment, I was all but immobilized by fear. But I never allowed my fear to stop me. I acknowledged the presence of the fear, often even talking to it: "I'm not going anywhere, so if you have something to tell me or teach me, you'd better get on with it!" I learned to use fear as fuel, and as a result became an adrenalin junkie. I thrived on fear, which is how I was able to face everything that confronted me! I realized this is where true unrecognizable transformation lived.

In 2000, my father, Peter Robert Anderson, died of prostate cancer, after having been sick for some time. He had experienced a remission, so we thought he was going to be all right. Alas, it didn't turn out this way. To lose my dad was a significant event in my life, since he was my rock—and I am definitely my father's daughter. He was a visionary, pioneer, and legacy leader, contributing hugely throughout his life to the youth industry, schooling system, and latterly aqua culture in New Zealand (before anyone truly knew what aqua culture was). An only child, he wanted to give his kids opportunities he never had—an aim he achieved. My mom and dad were married for forty years before he died, and to this day their marriage remains an inspiration to me. I so miss my father. But like my brother Mark, I know he walks with me daily. We are a formidable team, my dad, my bro., and I!

On one occasion, I was seconded to an international program across two continents and was based in The Netherlands, accountable for offices in Dordrecht, The Hague, and on to Boston, and New York. Within ten days of my arrival in The Netherlands, the president of the organization asked me to assume accountability for the rollout of a global restructuring. I can tell you, my fear was immense. But I chose to embrace it, as a result of which the assignment wasn't just extremely successful but life-altering, teaching me the power of belief in myself.

It was in The Netherlands that I took up meditation. In a country where I couldn't speak the language, there were few distractions outside my work, so I finally allowed myself to experience what it means to be one with All That Is.

While I was working with a group of senior executives in New York during the course of relocating the program office from The Netherlands to Boston, my office was five blocks from the World Trade Center. On September 10, 2001, I had the day off and contemplated going up the Twin Towers. While enjoying a cappuccino in the Hilton at the base of the towers, I decided to travel to Boston a day early. Being in the United States when the September 11 trauma hit changed my life. It woke me up to a sense of urgency: If I wasn't doing what I wanted to be doing, then what was the point of it all?

When I returned to New Zealand, I resigned from my position as Senior Program Director and embarked on one of the scariest ventures of my life, going out on my own in my career. "Fear" doesn't come close to describing what I felt when I took this step. With no roadmap, no "how to" manual, no mentor, and no support, it was just me and my belief in what I was meant to do with my life.

Someone commented recently, "You were courageous going out on your own in a completely new vocation with no real experience in that vocation."

I responded, "I was more terrified of what would happen if I didn't listen to the incessant internal voice that kept telling me to go out on my own." Going out on my own had little to do with starting my own company. It had everything to do with embracing my true identity.

I had invested a lot of money in my personal development but had struggled with sustaining change. I had also seen millions of corporate dollars invested in change programs that, three to five years from the time of implementation, reaped zero real return. Consequently, I was fascinated with the concept of sustainability, both at an individual and a corporate level. With this in mind, I launched Stepping Out, my own coaching practice, and dedicated the next three years to researching the elusive concept of sustainability.

I was so in debt at the time I launched my own business that I again chose to housesit to save money. How was it possible that I'd earned fairly good money over the years, yet continually struggled financially? Due to my low self-worth, I was unable to be with financial prosperity. To keep money I earned would have meant I was worth it, but I didn't really believe I was worth it. In fact, it took years for me to understand the direct relationship between self-worth and money. After all, money is just a form of energy. I honor my financial journey now because it was the only area of my life in which I wasn't in control and hence the one avenue Spirit had to access me. In the end, it gave me my biggest gift: I learned to trust.

It was three or four months before clients began arriving. When they did, I met them in a café or a hotel lobby. In the intervening months after my launch, I put myself through the wringer because nothing shifted. In the depths of extreme fear, with all my safety mechanisms out of the way, it was me and the unknown. I soon learned that I had never trusted the unknown. Now I truly met my Maker.

In those dark moments, I said to the ether: "You got me here and I'm not going anywhere. Whatever it is you want me to face, bring it on." Still, day after day, nothing shifted, and I cried tears that came from the depths of my soul. After years of being a control freak, this aspect of me was crumbling.

During this time, I learned that if we operate over the top of *any* personal issue, we will attract people and situations—in my case, a client base—that mirror our issues.

I also learned what it means to transform one's understanding of what we perceive as a breakdown. What looks awful can be a precursor to a break*through*. So now when things seem like a breakdown, I see this as an opportunity to celebrate, for I know the breakthrough will be just around the corner.

Going out on my own certainly put me in the foothills of the Himalayas. Yet this was not my Everest.

embodied self-love

I was thirty-seven years old and had battled with my weight for eighteen years. Now it was time to turn things around. I signed up for a new program called the Body For Life challenge, designed by Bill Phillips and developed in the United States, in which participants lose weight and increase fitness over a twelve-week period. In 2002, three-quarters of a million entrants took part in a worldwide challenge. Sixty of the 2,000 finalists were from New Zealand and I was one of them. I came down from 26% body fat to 15% and lost 21 pounds.

In those twelve weeks, I learned I had lacked a vital relationship with my spoken word. Until I followed this program, I hadn't been aware that I basically cheated on every diet I undertook. In completing the Body For Life challenge, I discovered I could accomplish anything my heart truly desired simply by practicing integrity with my word.

It's a strange experience being in the body as it comes down in size over such a short period. It's also a transformational experience.   It meant I was brought face to face with one of my great fears: being noticed because of a terrific body. How would I relate to myself now? How would others relate to me? Would I be able to handle those I attracted?

I was then approached to consider taking on the even greater challenge of competing in a body sculpting competition. After years of hiding my body, can you imagine what it was to take on such a feat? This was like shedding a skin that had covered me for decades. I had to learn to pose, choreograph a dance routine, and get down to 8% body fat.

I wanted to know what it felt like to have a body I admired. To accomplish this, I was forced to overcome my internal dialogue, given that most of the workouts were in front of mirrors or my personal trainer, which meant someone was critiquing my every move. Also, through body sculpting, I phased out my dependence on alcohol. It was at this time I also started to realize I couldn't expect someone to love me if I didn't love myself. I realized that for me this must start with my body, which led to a conviction that I needed to enter a phase of celibacy.

My body was my Everest, an area of my life in which I needed mastery.

One week before the competition, my personal trainer informed me that if I didn't get my choreographed routine right, I wouldn't be able to compete. A beautiful friend who realized what I was facing invited me around to her place, put on some soulful music, and asked me to close my eyes, requesting that I simply stand and be with the music, which I did for what felt like five minutes. Then she approached me as if to start a waltz and said, "Keep your eyes shut and just feel the music." We danced for ten or fifteen minutes, eyes closed, moving to the ebb and flow of the sounds. What a gift she gave me that day! I experienced joy in my body, learning what it means to know the oneness of being, similar to what one experiences in a meditative state.

It was then I realized what was missing from my choreographed routine: I wasn't there. Just as in my early attempts at public speaking, I was missing in action.

To express myself through my body when I had so disowned it meant I had to reintegrate with it and be *in* it for the first time since I was sixteen. Someone once said to me: "Sally, there's only one home, and that's our internal home." Nothing outside ourselves can give us the solace found within.

Dancing with my friend, I came home to my body that day, embracing my sixteen-year-old self and apologizing to myself for two decades of abuse.

The following week, I walked out on stage wearing six-inch high-heeled shoes, in a bikini that would barely cover your big toe, in front of 500 people. I carried out the posing techniques, completed the choreographed routine, and came away with an award for second place in my division.

When we've never done something before and have no idea how it's going to feel, the terror we experience can be paralyzing. However, the ecstasy that lies on the other side of our terror is invigorating. To walk this planet knowing what life is like beyond extreme terror is akin to walking on water.

When we attempt something we never thought we could do and succeed, we're left with an unreal sensation. The question that arises is: "Now what?" We have to learn how to relate to our new identity.

The combination of all I learned during my sixteen-year corporate experience, followed by going out on my own and coupled with the body-sculpting experience, led me to relate to myself in a new way.

It had been a long journey of reintegrating back into being whole and complete. I had come to realize there was nothing to fix. All that was required was to recognize and embrace who I had really been all along.

Chapter 19

everything is in perfection

Though we talk about the concept of the law of attraction, we really don't want to own that we attract experiences into our life consistent with how we feel about ourselves.

My self-loathing started at the age of three and it just got big, better, and best. To manifest a gang rape was simply a way to validate my self-hatred.

Yes, I'm saying I had a part to play in what transpired. Did I have a choice to hitchhike that day? Did I have a choice to walk into a public bar at the age of sixteen? My crime may have been naiveté, a product of my unconsciousness, but I nevertheless chose it. I put myself in a situation that was unsafe.

Life isn't doing it to us. Spirit isn't doing it to us.

Most people think life *is* doing it to us. For instance, women say to me, "What do you mean, I play a part in attracting miscarriages to me?"

I say to them, "When you are resonating with beliefs such as 'I'm terrified of childbirth,' 'I don't think I would be a good mother,' or 'I'm afraid of bringing a child into the world when I can't guarantee it will be safe,' what makes you think your body is going to give you a child?"

I've had women come to me wanting to have a child after working in the corporate world for twenty years, the whole time feeding their belief, "I don't want to have a child," and making sure everyone in their life knows this. "I do not want to have a baby" is a pretty stern affirmation to feed yourself. By the time you tell your body this for twenty years, you're pretty well programmed.

One woman insisted for years that she never wanted to get married and never wanted to have a child. With no time for "touchy-feely stuff," she was highly intentional about her corporate career in a masculine world that had no place for femininity either in her manner or in the way she dressed. She enrolled everybody in her belief she didn't want to get married. Then one day she met a man with whom she fell in love and who wanted to marry her.

I've found that people who say they don't want to get married and don't want children are often those who want these things the most, but who are also the most afraid.

Once settled in their new home, this woman began to long for a child to complement the dream. After several miscarriages, she couldn't understand why what she now wanted so badly was evading her.

The body has cellular memory. If we've trained our body for decades, as I did my own body through my self-hatred, we might address it at an intellectual level but we aren't dealing with it on a cellular level. It took five years of intense healing to remove the energy of the gang members who abused me.

We're like a computer software program. The program codes the computer. If we want to see a different experience on the computer monitor, we have to change the program because it won't change of its own accord but will keep on running endlessly. When we have damaged ourselves with a program that denies our true being, healing becomes necessary before we can attract what we want.

Have a look at your own life. How many years have you fed your story? What would life be like if you were no longer impacted by your story? Who would you be? What could you accomplish? To be a victim is just a technique for getting attention.

ending our victim story

Do you know what it's like for a seventy-five-year-old woman, who in six and a half decades has never expressed what happened to her as a young girl, to sit in the back of one of my seminars when I acknowledge the Mongrel Mob for my ability to lead an extraordinary life? You can understand why she would feel like getting up and leaving the room.

A lot of us would prefer to go to our grave never healing what happened to us because we are had by shame. Shame kills the spirit. It's the ultimate act of martyrdom. If you feel resistant to this conversation, I understand why. Some 6.8 billion people on the planet experience the same resistance, which is why there are so many people in the world who are in constant pain!

When I first found my own voice at the age of thirty, for at least five years I used it as a conversation stopper. To shock people was my way of getting my own back on society. In an intentionally manipulative way, I used my story to whack people. It was a "f..k you!" I may as well have had "don't f..k with me" tattooed on my forehead.

Few victims see their experience as perfect. Depending on the degree of trauma, they fuel their drama to keep it alive. When someone becomes aware they have played an integral role in keeping their story alive, inflicting pain on themselves in an ongoing way, they often choose to stay with the known world of their drama, instead of transforming their life, because it has become their default identity.

Friends or counselors who are willing to continue listening to a victim's story week after week, month after month, and even year after year, not only don't serve these individuals well, they often have an investment in keeping the individual's story going. As long as we believe in the power of victimhood, maintaining someone in their victim status justifies our own failure to show up to the full extent of our capabilities.

A lot of practitioners can't cut through victimhood because they aren't strong enough to stand up for the individual's true being. This is a barometer of their *own* development. The reason I'm able to partner people in having life-altering breakthroughs is that I go where no one else has gone to get the results nobody else has gotten. It takes courage to call to account a victim who has fed their victimhood for ten, twenty, or thirty years. But when someone stands up for them to the degree I stand up for them—stands up for who they *really* are—a single conversation can shift them into an entirely new place. I have watched people shift in almost no time at all when I tell them, "If you want to tell your story, save yourself some money. If you want to get beyond your story, let's get on with it." People realize that far from being powerless, they are a person of unlimited power. To see them no longer hurting after being in agony for years excites me.

We can be so swayed by a person's professional qualifications that we imagine what they say "goes." If we aren't strong enough in ourselves, we can end up being committed. There's more to somebody's state of mind than a checklist of behavioral symptoms. I ask myself how many people in psychiatric units shouldn't actually be there. I now advise my clients that if they seek any kind of professional opinion, they should first identify for themselves what's happening. Then when they receive a professional opinion, they can check it against their own affirmative knowing, because we *always* know. This statement may alarm some people, including some professionals, but I believe in the innate insight of the human spirit.

I look back on this experience now and see the perfection of it. All is always in perfection. Some people find it hard to relate to the idea that everything is always in perfection. But as I have evolved, I have become more and more aware of how everything truly is in perfection. Everything that happens in our life is intended to provide us with an opportunity to move more fully into our true identity.

On the block at age sixteen, the Mongrel Mob were my spiritual initiators to fulfill my purpose of helping change the way the human psyche works on the planet. I'm clear I wouldn't be here today were it not for this purpose.

Can you appreciate why I can acknowledge the Mongrel Mob for facilitating me in leading an extraordinary life? Can you see the perfection? The odds of somebody going through such an experience with no support and coming out the way I have are huge. So you tell me, has everything not been perfect?

I would like you to entertain looking at your own circumstances off the back of what I've shared about my own life. Maybe, just maybe, everything you have experienced in your life to-date has been supremely perfect for your development into the unique person you, and only you, have the potential to be.

I can now acknowledge my parents. Thanks Mom and Dad for not supporting me in the way I yearned for. Had you done so, I would never have learned what I learned and wouldn't be doing what I'm doing today.

transformation unlike i had ever seen

In year four of my coaching practice Stepping Out, I decided to set up a seminar company and a coach training school. Having never been formally trained, it had been a leap to set up my own coaching practice, let alone my own seminar company and coach training school. My passion was fuelled by the transformation I was witnessing in those I was privileged to coach. I wanted to reach more people with the approach I had developed.

I decided to bring outside investors into the business to run these aspects of the company, while I embarked on furthering my keynote speaking career. All investors had experienced my approach and believed in the vision. Probably for the first time in my life, I now understood what it meant to be supported in business. I commuted between Auckland, New Zealand, and Sydney, Australia, for eighteen months. I met a man, who runs an organization called Thoughtleaders, he continues to be the leading keynote speaker in Australia. He gave me the gift of truly being seen and heard in a way I had never experienced. Throughout my Thoughtleader journey, I was privileged to meet some of Australasia's leading thought leaders, and to this day I feel privileged to have come to know such pioneering individuals, many of whom remain soul friends. Nevertheless, I was still not fully healed, with a gaping need for external validation. It was humbling to admit that I was a "try hard" who didn't truly feel I had what it takes

I returned to New Zealand to find the businesses weren't in good shape, and it wasn't long before both companies folded and I lost my entire financial investment. My relationship with my investment partners turned to custard, and once again I was face-to-face with yet another dark night of the soul experience.

death of the ego

I have learned that death of the ego happens in five phases:

- **Phase 1 Denial:** Not wanting to face what's happening.

- **Phase 2 Fear:** Facing up to what it is we are denying.

- **Phase 3 Victimhood:** Feeling powerless to change the situation.

- **Phase 4 Anger:** Why me, when all I do is give?

- **Phase 5 Acceptance:** Realizing that all is in perfection.

It took me two years to work through this process and reach a level of acceptance, to the point I had at last returned home to myself. I now have compassion for what transpired and accept that it had to happen for me to truly understand what it means to live an integrated life. You can't put a price tag on this kind of learning.

I had to lose everything to gain everything. There was no other way Spirit could get my attention. During this time, I experienced many episodes of the dark night of the soul, which in due course led me to Gerard May's life-altering book *Dark Night Of The Soul*. This made an impact on me like no other book I had ever read, which is really saying something for a gal who read every self-help book on the market during more than two and a half decades. May explains:

> … The dark night is a profoundly good thing. It is an ongoing spiritual process in which we are liberated from attachments and compulsions and empowered to live and love more freely. Sometimes this letting go of old ways is painful, occasionally even devastating. But this is not why the night is called "dark". The darkness of the night implies nothing sinister, only that the liberation takes place in hidden ways, beneath our knowledge and understanding. It happens mysteriously, in secret, and beyond our conscious control. For that reason it can be disturbing or even scary, but in the end it always works to our benefit.

During this two-year period of dying to my egoic identity, I kicked and screamed all the way, not realizing that it was my desperate need to retain control that was denying me evolution as a spiritual being. My growth took the fast track when I attended a ten-day meditational retreat called Vipassanna, which can be found all over the world and serves to teach westerners how to meditate. Can you imagine yours truly in an environment in which you aren't allowed to speak for ten days and can't have eye-contact with anyone? Plus, you are expected to meditate for ten-to-twelve hours a day. It took until day six for me to realize why I was there, and it happened while I was watching a discourse of the leader Goenka. The discourse had a cathartic effect on me, and I realized I hadn't yet owned my true being and what I was meant to do in life.

I wouldn't change a thing about my journey, because every bit of it is what brought me where I am today. I have always been impatient, but Spirit in its wisdom always knows the best course for each of us, and the timing in my case has been impeccable. My work now is an extension of who I choose to be in the world.

fulfilling a lifetime dream

In May of 2009, I fulfilled another lifetime dream, marrying Roger, a staunchly Maori man (the indigenous culture of New Zealand) who rocked my world. I met him a year earlier at an event called a Wananga, which is Maori for a family gathering. At the Wananga I had the privilege to facilitate 3 days of healing with Roger's entire Whanau ('family' in maori). Can you imagine what it is like to be with the man of your dreams when you have coached most of his family members. During this experience I coached Roger in my professional capacity and as a result something significant happened. Spirit intervened and brought us together. I will never forget the first moment I saw him, for he exuded such a presence. He is the strongest, most intelligent, culturally attuned, powerful, caring, spiritual man I have ever met.

Roger had never dated what the Maori call a "pakeha," a white person. We are a bi-cultural couple, and it was evident from our first meeting we were destined to be together. Perhaps our dual journey can help bridge the divide between indigenous cultures and the mainstream. It was after watching the *60 Minutes* documentary about my ordeal Roger knew he wanted to marry me. At the time of this writing, we have already celebrated our first wedding anniversary.

Chapter 19

f r e e f a l l

When you've experienced terror of the kind I experienced at age sixteen, you walk in shoes like no other.

I believe my journey has prepared me to share with people how they can come only from love, listen to the people in their lives for their greatness, and be a contribution, until this becomes the new norm in human societies.

Can you imagine such a world?

I can because I have experienced it in my own life.

People can't comprehend how we could avoid adversity because they just accept that to hurt is part of the human condition. The journey into higher consciousness outlined in this book needs, I believe, to be adopted in our educational system to ensure future generations live a more evolved, enlightened existence. If we operated at a high level of consciousness on a global basis, we would no longer need adversity in order to learn. How will we evolve as a species if we don't teach the evolution of higher consciousness in our schools?

a life in which fear no longer "has" you

I delivered a keynote address and ran a workshop with managers from a mental health and disability center. Off the back of my sharing in the keynote, I became a catalyst for people to find their voice for the first time. In the break, fifteen people requested one-on-one coaching. The depth of what they shared was profound. Each of them prefaced what they were going to say by telling me, "I have never told this to anyone before."

The first person was a man who was about 120 pounds overweight, though still extremely handsome. He had been involved with the Mongrel Mob five years earlier but had left the gang and got off drugs. The father of five young children, he lived in fear the mob would put a hit out on him. "How do you deal with such fear?" he asked.

I posed the question, "Do you have a faith?"

"I'm alive today because of my faith," he said.

"If you are in tune with your faith," I pressed, "do you believe anybody can actually 'get you?'"

"No," he said, as the depth of what I was suggesting sank in.

"Then your fear of a mob hit is the only thing that can attract the actuality of a hit," I explained.

If we walk our faith, nothing can get to us. Only that which is aligned with our purpose can occur in our lives.

This doesn't mean we might not be killed like Gandhi or imprisoned like Nelson Mandela. The point is that they were fearless in the face of situations that would terrify most of us. They didn't live in fear of something happening to them because they realize the only things that could happen were those that would fulfill their purpose. This was the clear teaching of Jesus as he faced his crucifixion.

Every morning for the past five years, this former mob member had been fueling his fear that if he wasn't with his family, they might be unsafe. His entire resonance was fear-based, with safety his preoccupation.

When we discussed what he had been making all of this mean, he said, "I don't deserve this. I've straightened my life out. I'm now being responsible for my family. Why can't they leave me alone? I've done my time."

As we talked, it became clear his terror actually stemmed from childhood when his peers pressured him to join the mob in the first place. As he became present to the fact he was the one attracting fear, he realized he had a choice:

he could feed his faith instead of feeding his fear. In other words, he had been giving his faith lip service rather than living it 24/7.

Fear is not a spiritual practice.

embracing the unknown

Let me tell you about two clients whose anxiety states were identical. This example continues to teach me that circumstances have no reality but the reality we give them.

One client owed the IRS a half-million dollars. Imagine his anxiety!

The other client was experiencing an *equal* level of anxiety because she was waiting for the bill for her Visa card, on which she had a credit limit of $2,000 and which she hardly ever used. The monthly payment was $20, yet she was watching the mail daily for it to arrive so she could pay it immediately because it made her anxious to have *anything* on her card.

How is it possible that the anxiety states of these two people were identical?

These examples show us vividly how it isn't our circumstances that create our state of mind. Our circumstances only elicit *what's already inside us.*

It's *never* the situation but *always* the meaning we add to it.

By connecting to who we really are in our essence, where we are one with our Source, we begin to imagine ourselves differently from the fearful, anxious person we have known ourselves to be. Reimagining ourselves, we move forward based on our new level of awareness. I'm interested in people stepping outside the confines of what limits them so that the sides fall away, the bottom falls out, and the individual experiences being *at one with the unknown as a way of being.* To be at one with the unknown then becomes the norm.

To the unconscious mind, the known world feels safe, whereas to the conscious mind the unknown is safe. How many people do you know who focus on the unknown? Imagine if focusing on the unknown were a core curriculum in schools! It should be at least as important to learn mastery of fear, and hence of the inner critic that fear triggers, as it is to learn to read and write.

Most people don't relate to self-mastery, which is about discipline, as freeing. But discipline and freedom unequivocally go together, for it's only through disciplining ourselves we can become free. Indeed, discipline is the access point to freedom. For instance, consider how mastery of our fear allows us to enjoy freedom from self-constraint. Mastery of issues, problems, and challenges frees us from anxiety and enables us to experience peace. Mastery of our inner critic frees us to access our potential. Mastery of confusion frees us from indecision so we have clarity, purpose, and direction.

It took discipline to keep going down the road my heart wanted to travel when I could see no evidence it was bearing fruit. But this self-discipline was ultimately to realize my dream of living my legacy.

beliefs are wishful thinking—faith is intuitive knowing

When we talk a lot about what we believe, it's usually because we have little real *knowing*.

Those who walk their faith instead of just talking it emanate a sense of knowing. Indeed, the more we surrender to the unknown and simply *trust,* the more the universe provides us with awareness.

As our inner knowing kicks in, the more receptive we become to the energies that flood the world. Our sensory perception is heightened—taste, touch, smell, hearing, sight—and our clairvoyant ability increases. Knowing becomes our way of operating in the whole of life, which enables us to become our own authority.

Safety can only truly be experienced through faith. Having said this, it matters a great deal how we understand faith. I'm not talking about a set of doctrinal declarations, even though these may have their place. As I've already intimated, when I use the word "faith," I'm speaking of *trust*. Humans are innately trusting, but many of us have learned not to trust—so much so that distrust has become a universal phenomenon. Nevertheless, distrust runs contrary to our essential nature.

We were born implicitly trusting the unknown but we have forgotten how to do so. Between the ages of three and five, we learned to adopt certain beliefs and values—"don't touch this, don't do that"—that define what's acceptable and what's not acceptable, which then frame the way we administer our life. An important aspect of my work is to give people permission to access their unknown but essential being. They then learn to trust themselves—to believe in *themselves* instead of in a set of concepts called "beliefs."

Most of us have to be forced to change because the reality is we don't trust the unknown and are terrified of going into *freefall* were we ever to abandon ourselves to the unknown. The nemesis of humanity is our terror of losing control.

nothing to fear

To enter into a world free of emotional and psychological pain, we must embrace freefall.

To visually express freefall, I use the image of a white feather against a black background because access to the light is through the dark. The imagery invites us to go to the places we don't want to go because this is how we liberate our soul. When we do this, we realize there was nothing frightening there at all.

A feather is soft and gentle with many dimensions of intricacy. Feathers fall gracefully and effortlessly. Freefall can either be a helter-skelter, terrifying experience, or a graceful way of being with All That Is.

A feather travels in the air to many destinations, totally trusting the unknown. Once we let go and trust the unknown, we experience true freedom.

A feather also floats in silence, which is one of the most powerful forms of communication.

A falling feather dances with gravity. It doesn't buck reality but goes with the flow of the real world.

Feathers give birds the gift of flight, and flight is about freedom without constraints as we pursue a clear sense of purpose.

A feather is light but has a design that's scientifically complex and a form that's truly beautiful. We too are complex in design. Once we embrace what we perceive to be dark about us, we experience everything as light.

A falling feather is a wonderful metaphor for life. Once we give ourselves fully to our life, we are propelled wherever we need to go.

It takes courage to embark on a journey without knowing our destination. But if we are honest, this is exactly how life is. We really don't know where it's going, much as we try to control, mash, pummel, and force it into a certain shape.

If we trust, we will find a way for our intellect and heart to work together, and then the whole of our being will be at our disposal to achieve whatever our purpose is.

In my own life, I clung to the cliff face for many years because I trusted no one. I now know that letting go and experiencing freefall means experiencing love at its ultimate level, for love is limitless.

about the author

Sally Anderson is Australasia's Foremost Thinkers In Sustainable Transformation. As one of the most cutting edge Leadership Coaches, Inspirational Speakers, Seminar Leaders, Master Coach Trainers, Sally has inspired thousands of people from feeling disempowered in their personal and professional lives to experiencing outstanding sustainable results.

Sally is passionate about the advancement of human performance and is pioneering new ways of being in human consciousness through providing revolutionary education. With her trademark passion and stalwart commitment, Sally is committed to "sharing her wealth of knowledge", spreading her message to an ever-increasing audience by taking the mystery out of achieving sustainable results.

One of the leading Inspirational Female Speakers of our time Sally has a powerful story to share – she entertains, educates, and transforms. She gains the hearts and minds of her audience with a message that impacts long after her presentation ends. Her story resonates with all who hear her speak and their outlook on life is transformed forever!

There are key note speakers who entertain, some who educate, and others who inform. Sally Anderson transforms!.

Her personal brand of storytelling resonates with all types of audiences, revealing not only her expertise, but the passion for the subject she speaks about. Audience evaluations consistently rate her presentations as exceptional and life-altering!

Audiences are left in no doubt as to her message and the difference it can make in their lives. You will see Sally building a close rapport with your audience using her innovative and refreshing approach to keynote speaking, and sharing her unbelievable journey.

"I hear many speakers and their stories, having operated a speaker bureau for over five years, however few really touched me as profoundly as Sally Anderson's story. Sally's story has you gripping to your chair, it takes you to a place where you cannot even dare to imagine. However she brings you back gently and you let go of the gut wrenching as you learn how this remarkable woman brought herself back from the depths of darkness to move on to embrace life. Sally has the power to capture your audience and give them life changing tools in as little as an hour. Since I heard Sally speak and I have never forgotten her story or message. A true inspiration."

Debbie Carr, Director True Colours Keynotes/Sydney-Australia

To discuss hiring Sally Anderson as the keynote for your next event or conference, contact her direct via www.sally-anderson.com

As Founder of Sally Anderson International Limited and Freefall International Limited Sally has shared her proprietary Freefall Education® strategies at retreats/ seminars for more than 10 years. Should you be interested in any of the services within her portfolio please contact her c/- of the websites outlined below:

1. Cutting Edge Leadership Coaching

2. Leadership Retreats

3. Inspirational Keynote Speaking

WEB www.sally-anderson.com / BLOG www.sally-andersonblog.com

Living Life Beyond The Edge

1. Freefall 3 Day Public Seminars

2. Freefall 3 Day Corporate Customized Seminars

3. Freefall 12 Week Coach Certification

WEB www.freefallexperience.com / BLOG www.freefallselfimprovement.com

Contact Address:
Sally Anderson International Limited & Freefall International Limited
PO Box 91770
Victoria Street West
Auckland 1142
NEW ZEALAND
Email: support@sally-anderson.com
Phone: 1+64 9 488 6768

FREE RESOURCES

We are committed to exceeding expectations and offering real value with all the services we provide so please feel free to subscribe to the FREE resource below:-

BLOG www.sally-andersonblog.com

BLOG www.freefallselfimprovement.com

BUY A SHARE OF THE FUTURE IN YOUR COMMUNITY

These certificates make great holiday, graduation and birthday gifts that can be personalized with the recipient's name. The cost of one S.H.A.R.E. or one square foot is $54.17. The personalized certificate is suitable for framing and will state the number of shares purchased and the amount of each share, as well as the recipient's name. The home that you participate in "building" will last for many years and will continue to grow in value.

Here is a sample SHARE certificate:

THIS CERTIFIES THAT

YOUR NAME HERE

HAS INVESTED IN A HOME FOR A DESERVING FAMILY

1985-2010

TWENTY-FIVE YEARS OF BUILDING FUTURES
IN OUR COMMUNITY ONE HOME AT A TIME

1200 SQUARE FOOT HOUSE @ $65,000 = $54.17 PER SQUARE FOOT
This certificate represents a tax deductible donation. It has no cash value.

YES, I WOULD LIKE TO HELP!

*I support the work that Habitat for Humanity does and I want to be part of the excitement! As a donor, I will receive periodic updates on your construction activities but, more importantly, I know my gift will help a family in our community realize the dream of homeownership. **I would like to SHARE in your efforts against substandard housing in my community!** (Please print below)*

PLEASE SEND ME _____ SHARES at $54.17 EACH = $ $_____

In Honor Of: _____

Occasion: (Circle One)   *HOLIDAY   BIRTHDAY   ANNIVERSARY*

   OTHER: _____

Address of Recipient: _____

Gift From: _____ *Donor Address:* _____

Donor Email: _____

I AM ENCLOSING A CHECK FOR $ $_____ PAYABLE TO HABITAT FOR HUMANITY <u>OR</u> PLEASE CHARGE MY VISA OR MASTERCARD *(CIRCLE ONE)*

Card Number _____ Expiration Date: _____

Name as it appears on Credit Card _____ Charge Amount $ _____

Signature _____

Billing Address _____

Telephone # Day _____ Eve _____

PLEASE NOTE: Your contribution is tax-deductible to the fullest extent allowed by law.
Habitat for Humanity • P.O. Box 1443 • Newport News, VA 23601 • 757-596-5553
www.HelpHabitatforHumanity.org

CPSIA information can be obtained at www.ICGtesting.com
Printed in the USA
BVOW040744251011

274411BV00003B/2/P